What about me?

An Equal Opportunities Support Pack
for

The National Standards for Under Eights Day Care and Childminding
NVQs in Early Years Care and Education
NVQs Playwork
NVQs in Caring for Children and Young People
Early Years and Childcare Quality Assurance Scheme Kitemarks

by

Erica Thomas

East Riding College
Learning Resources Centres
T: 01262 455060
E: lrcenquiries@eastridingcollege.ac.uk

Published by:
HLB Associates

Further copies may be obtained from:
HLB Associates

07976 605034
E-mail: hlb@hlbassociates.plus.com

ISBN No. 0 9547362 0 6

Printed by: PWD-The Creative Solution
01772 312554
info@pwdesignuk.co.uk

Foreword

Equal opportunities is a challenging and complex subject and all early years practitioners, whether they work in care or education, have to work towards and practice equal opportunities. The National Standards for Under Eights Day Care and Childminding, which all non-maintained early years providers are inspected against, clearly state the registered person and all staff have to actively promote equality of opportunity and anti-discriminatory practice for **all** children. The supporting criteria for Standard 9 (Equal Opportunities) explains that all early years providers have to:

- have, and regularly review, an equal opportunities policy (although not mandatory for childminders, many early years professionals consider an equal opportunities policy good practice, as it helps to prove understanding of equal opportunities issues)

- treat children and adults with equal concern, having regard to relevant anti-discriminatory good practice; along with promoting equal opportunities with regard to employment, training, admissions and access to resources, activities and facilities available

- liaise with parents to ensure all children's records contain information which enables appropriate care to be given

Teachers in the maintained sector have to work within an equal opportunities framework; and the occupational competences underpinning the national vocational qualifications (NVQ) that many practitioners hold, or are working towards, indicate a commitment to equal opportunities is essential to good practice. Also, early years providers working towards the achievement of a quality assurance scheme kitemark have to demonstrate how they have met equal opportunities quality standards.

The European Union Council Employment Directive on Equal Treatment requires all member states to introduce legislation prohibiting direct and indirect discrimination at work on the grounds of age, disability, religion or belief, and sexual orientation. The British government has accepted this directive (commonly known as the Employment Directive), which establishes a general framework for equal treatment in employment and vocational training and guidance, ensuring there will be minimum standards for combating discrimination throughout the European Union. Consequently, the government intends to introduce new anti-discrimination legislation in time to meet the deadlines agreed in the Employment Directive, that is, 2003 for sexual orientation and religion, and 2006 for age. Age legislation will be in place by December 2004 so people will have two years to prepare for the changes.

This pack provides background information as to why you would want to actively engage in and promote equal opportunities, even if there was no regulation or legislation that forced you to do so. Also, even if you have attended equal opportunities training previously, or covered it as part of a training course, both acceptable and good practice may well have changed.

As all early years practitioners are at different stages in their knowledge, understanding and practice, the pack provides an overview which should make you more aware of what you already know, introduce you to new ideas and give you more confidence to apply equal opportunities in your work situation. It will help to clarify what equal opportunities is about and hopefully give you more confidence in an area of early years work that some practitioners find threatening.

The information provided is at an introductory level. It introduces readers to terminology, the context (including legislative background) within which equal opportunities works in the United Kingdom (UK) and provides an outline of the scope of equal opportunities at the beginning of the 21st century. It can also be used by those with some knowledge as a reminder of the wide ranging nature of equal opportunities. It is ideal to use as a precursor to face to face training.

The pack focuses on general equal opportunities issues and so is as pertinent to the general role of businesses/organisations as to the provision of childcare and early years education. Therefore, it will be useful for voluntary groups including out of school clubs. However, it is not a substitute for training relevant to employment law or the legal aspects of employment. Please note, the term 'early years' is used to cover early years education, early years education and childcare, childcare, playwork, out of school care, and childminders. Also note, the term 'children' includes young people.

It may be that the reader personally identifies with one or more of the categories outlined in the 'What about me?' section. Rather than this being seen as a threat, it is hoped this identification will make readers appreciate the extent of the application of equal opportunities and the importance of its promotion, particularly if they have personally experienced discrimination, although they may have been unaware of this at the time.

Working towards equal opportunities is a continuing and continual process which takes place over time and is assisted by reflective practice. This pack provides an opportunity for practitioners to think and rethink equal opportunities perspectives and the relevant underlying principles. Readers are encouraged to use the space provided to jot down thoughts and feelings as this makes a significant contribution to reflective practice. In understanding the principles behind equal opportunities, practitioners will be able to ensure they adapt to changes in good practice and assist everyone to achieve their potential.

Contents

Acknowledgments

The help and support of the following people is gratefully acknowledged:

Susan Atherton
Andrea Cawley
Janet Davies
Catherine Garner
Corinne Peters
Debbie Tomkins

Also Paul Williams of PWD.

Common Equal Opportunities Terminology

Discrimination - treating someone less favourably than others, either directly or indirectly

Inclusion - this applies to everyone and is particularly used in reference to those who may be disadvantaged or at risk of discrimination. Within special educational needs the term refers to including such pupils in mainstream education

****

Harassment - any attention based on gender, sexual orientation, nationality, colour, ethnic group or disability which is unwanted, unreciprocated, uninvited, or offensive; such behaviour makes the recipient feel uncomfortable, fearful and embarrassed and they want it to stop; it can be verbal, visual or physical including:

- comments, jokes, abuse
- circulation of offensive images or literature
- offensive email or telephone calls
- physical contact, including assault
- requests for sexual favours
- intrusive behaviour

Prejudice - a pre-conceived opinion against or in favour of; bias or partiality; within equal opportunities work, prejudice is usually regarded as prejudging someone, knowing next to nothing about them but jumping to conclusions because of a characteristic, for example, appearance

Stereotype - a person or thing that conforms to an unjustifiably fixed, usually standardised, mental picture; the most common stereotypes found in text books and most equal opportunities training are: sex and gender, racial origins, cultural or social background (including religion, language, class and family pattern) and disability

Tokenism - pretending or appearing to value something when you do not; sometimes described as 'lip service'

****

Culture - the customs, civilisations and achievements of a particular time or people; the collective and dominant belief system of a group of people living close enough to influence one another

Creed - a system of religious belief or a faith

Disability – a physical or mental condition that limits a person's movements, senses (hearing, sight) or activities

Ethnic - relating to a group of people having a common national or cultural tradition; indicating origin by birth or descent, rather than by present nationality

Faith - a strong belief in a religion

Gender – the state of being female or male

Language - the method of communication either spoken or written, consisting of the use of words in an agreed way

Nationality - the status of belonging to a particular nation (which is a large number of people united by common descent, culture, or language inhabiting a particular geographic area)

Race - each of the major divisions of humankind, having distinct physical characteristics; a nation or group of people regarded by themselves or others as having a distinct ethnic origin

Religion - the belief in a superhuman controlling power especially in a personal God or Gods entitled to obedience and worship

Special Educational Needs (SEN) - learning difficulties that make it harder for the individual to learn than most others of the same age, such that extra or different help is required

Sexual orientation - this is sometimes referred to as sexuality and is usually taken to mean a person's sexual preference in respect of attraction to another

Bi-sexual - sexually attracted to both women and men

Heterosexual - sexually attracted to the opposite sex

Homosexual – sexually attracted to others of one's own sex. Currently in popular speech, 'gay' refers to sexual relationships between males and 'lesbian' sexual relationships between females. While many people think the term 'queer' is politically incorrect, be aware some homosexuals may prefer this term as they feel 'gay' or 'lesbian' is not an appropriate 'label' for them

Transsexual - a person identified as one sex at birth (usually based on visible sex characteristics) but later discovered to have the physical sex characteristics of the opposite sex. This often manifests itself by having emotional and psychological feelings considered to be more appropriate to the opposite sex. Medical investigation often reveals internal, physical characteristics that match more to the sex the person feels her/himself to be, rather than what her/his visible characteristics lead them to be identified as. Transsexuals may or may not choose to undergo surgery to align how they feel themselves to be with their physical characteristics

****

Ageism - the belief that there are characteristics, abilities or qualities specific to particular ages and, as some of these are valued more than others, generally youth is considered superior to age

Racism - the belief that there are characteristics, abilities or qualities specific to each race and as some of these are valued more than others, some races are superior to others. It is based on the false idea that some physical characteristics (for example, skin colour), or ethnic background, make some people better than others

Sexism - the belief that there are characteristics, abilities or qualities specific to each sex and as some of these are valued more than others, one sex is superior to another, (historically the male sex has been considered to be superior)

****

Anti-discrimination work - all people should acknowledge and address any personal beliefs or opinions which prevent them from respecting others. Plus, they need to comply with legislation and their workplace policies relating to discrimination. In addition, early years practitioners need to be mindful of the fact that children learn prejudice at a very early age, so must provide them with accurate information to help them avoid prejudice, as well as challenging all expressions of prejudice whether from children or adults, along with offering support to those who are objects of prejudice and discrimination

Celebrating diversity - this is one of the most common ways of demonstrating compliance with equal opportunities ideas. Many early years settings find providing information about a variety of traditions, customs and festivals is relatively easy, particularly if they operate in an ethnically diverse area. It can be argued this is even more important in areas where there are few members of minority ethnic groups and also that the term should not be confined to racial diversity. In addition, early years practitioners need to be mindful of helping children to develop a sense of identity within their racial, cultural and social groups as well as providing opportunities to learn about other cultures. It is worth remembering pride in one's own cultural and social background does not require condemnation of that of others

Equality of opportunity - having equal access to opportunities to learn and develop and so an individual can work towards realising her/his potential. The individuality of a person should be respected and therefore people should not be treated all the same; to meet individual needs, it is necessary to treat people with 'equal concern', giving the appropriate support (whether this be 'more' or 'different' support) to ensure equality of opportunity. Avoid stereotyping people on any basis, as stereotypes act as barriers to equality of access to opportunity. By actively demonstrating that you value individuals' personal characteristics you help her/him develop and maintain self-esteem

Introduction

There are many assumptions made when referring to equal opportunities work, not least that everyone will want to do this work because to do otherwise would not be right and so anyone choosing to ignore equal opportunities practice would be regarded as either ignorant, immoral, or both. This is based on the idea that equality is a universal concept, that is a set of rules, norms and principles, not only equally applicable to everyone, but also recognisable by, and acceptable to everyone. Another assumption is everyone knows and understands the terms and phrases used. None of these are particularly true. While many people work towards equal opportunities out of a genuine belief that each individual should have the chance to achieve her/his potential, some work towards equal opportunities out of fear of being different if they do otherwise, or because of the threat imposed by legislation. Equally, many people do not have a clear understanding of terms used; nor are they aware that, like most things in life, equal opportunities concepts evolve and therefore change.

The section on Common Equal Opportunities Terminology will help to clarify current terms and phrases. However, the evolutionary nature of the concepts can only be dealt with by remaining up to date, through attending training and reading current publications.

In the past, equal opportunities was seen as applying mainly to gender, that is equality between the sexes, or more often as a race issue. So much equal opportunities education and training was focused on multi-cultural work. However, equal opportunities is not just about recognising racial diversity and, unfortunately, multi-cultural education and training does not necessarily prevent discrimination or racism. We live in a society made up of different individuals and groups, although not all the groups are equally visible. This diversity needs to be acknowledged, valued, and respected. In doing so equal opportunities has to have a much wider meaning, it now involves and implies developing responses for any group facing disadvantage (social or economic deprivation) or social exclusion, and discrimination. Besides the more familiar sex, race, disability and age, equal opportunities practice needs to be applied to what are referred to as 'hard to reach' groups, for example, travellers, transient families, refugees, teenage parents, and people who are at risk of exclusion through poor access to transport.

Equal opportunities practice is not about treating everyone in the same way. All people are different, this is what makes them unique and individual. Unfortunately, focusing on differences between people can result in negative attitudes and assumptions which may lead to prejudice and discrimination. The fact that people are different does not mean they do not share some similarities; they are always similar in some respects and potentially share some characteristics, experiences and goals. Also, because they are different does not mean they are not of equal worth; they are different and equal. Equal opportunities practice is about giving everyone an equal chance to live free from prejudice and discrimination. In this context 'living' would include the rights to learn and work.

To ensure everyone has an equal chance, it is necessary to have an understanding of who may not experience equality and why, as well as understanding the terms that underpin all equal opportunities training and work, along with the legal requirements and regulations. Section 2 looks at different groups of people who may not experience equality; Section 3 provides an overview of current legislation; and Section 4 some general guidelines for equal opportunities practice. The following is an overview of the terms used in all equal opportunities training and work.

Prejudice is a pre-conceived opinion against or in favour of something, in other words, bias or partiality. Within equal opportunities work, prejudice is usually regarded as prejudging someone, knowing next to nothing about them but jumping to conclusions because of a characteristic, for example, appearance.

Attitudes, including prejudiced attitudes, are developed from experiences. Prejudice is often a reaction to a situation by people who feel threatened, even though they may not be aware they are afraid, or are unwilling to acknowledge their fear. In refusing to consider alternatives, that is having a closed mind, further experiences and encounters are likely to produce a hardening of attitudes, rather than generate change.

Discrimination is treating someone less favourably than others, either directly or indirectly. It damages everybody, though it does so in different ways. All those who experience discrimination, either as perpetrator or recipient, are disadvantaged by it as discrimination affects people's behaviour, confidence, motivation and ability to learn and develop. Discriminatory practice of any kind can result in a lack of ability to empathise, that is, understand the feelings of another; empathy is crucial to respecting and valuing each other.

For many people who experience prejudice and/or discrimination the consequences are low esteem and damage to their self identity. One way to avoid prejudice and discrimination is to address negative attitudes and assumptions in a positive way. This can be demonstrated by mutual respect and a willingness to consult and negotiate.

A **stereotype** is a person or thing that conforms to an unjustifiably fixed, usually standardised, mental picture. The most common stereotypes found in textbooks and most equal opportunities training are: sex and gender, racial origins, cultural or social background (including religion, language, class and family pattern) and disability.

Stereotyping people for any reason is not efficient or accurate when assessing performance, ability or potential and can be very deceptive, for example, believing all black people have a good sense of rhythm. There is no evidence for this, some black people have no better sense of rhythm than non-black people. All people are individuals and although experiences are a contributory factor in making them what they are, the primary factors are their interests, temperament and personality.

Harassment is any attention based on gender, sexual orientation, nationality, colour, ethnic group or disability which is unwanted, unreciprocated, uninvited, or offensive. Such behaviour makes the recipient feel uncomfortable, fearful and embarrassed and they want it to stop. The attention can be verbal, visual or physical including:

- comments, jokes, abuse
- circulation of offensive images or literature
- offensive email or telephone calls
- physical contact, including assault
- requests for sexual favours
- intrusive behaviour

The gap between acceptable behaviour and harassment can be very small.

Tokenism is pretending or appearing to value something when you do not; sometimes described as 'lip service'.

Many ideas and practices that evolved from multi-cultural training are now viewed as tokenistic, for example, having a black doll alongside the more usual white dolls. While dolls and other toys and images that reflect a diverse range of ethnic origins are a welcome sign in early years provision, they have to be used in context. Just having black dolls in the setting will not make children aware of equal opportunities, largely because equal opportunities is about far more that skin colour.

Equality of opportunity is about having equal access to opportunities to learn and develop, so an individual can work towards realising her/his potential. For a person to realise her/his potential, it is essential s/he feels a sense of pride in her/his identity. Thus the individuality of a person should be acknowledged, valued and respected, and people cannot be treated the same. To meet individual needs it is necessary to treat people with 'equal concern', giving the appropriate support (whether this be 'more' or 'different' support) to ensure equality of opportunity.

Demonstrating equal opportunities involves working in an evenhanded manner and applying accepted and common standards of good practice. Everyone should examine their own attitudes and evaluate the impact of these on others, but this is particularly important for those who work with children, as the nature of their work makes them role models. It is necessary to avoid stereotyping people on any basis, as stereotypes act as barriers to equality of access to opportunity. It is also important to understand, respect and value similarities and differences that exist between people. By actively demonstrating you value an individual's personal characteristics you help her/him develop and maintain self-esteem.

Reflection

What experience do I already have in respect of equal opportunities?

-
-
-

How confident do I feel about my equal opportunities practice?

-
-
-

How have I experienced prejudice, discrimination, harassment and/or stereotyping?

-
-
-

With whom can I discuss issues which concern me?

-
-
-

What about me?

This section looks at a wide range of categories to which equal opportunities applies. It provides some general information as a reminder why being in any of these categories may result in being disadvantaged (socially or economically deprived). Some of the categories overlap or interlink and so some people may find themselves experiencing more than one category at any one time. This is known as multiple disadvantage and is described in the final section.

Some of the circumstances described below may increase the vulnerability of some of those who experience them. A person is usually considered to be vulnerable when current, or immediately foreseeable, potential circumstances mean s/he is at risk of mental, physical, emotional, sexual or financial harm. Factors that can increase vulnerability include age, physical/mental condition (including depression), race, religion, colour, culture, sexual orientation, lack of care, and abusive relationships.

A common experience associated with prejudice and discrimination is for the recipient to feel stigmatized. Stigma and stigmatize are words that will arise frequently in the following descriptions and can be defined as:

- stigma – a mark of disgrace associated with a particular circumstances, quality or person

- stigmatize – regard as worthy of disgrace

It is important to remember while categories (or labels) can be very useful in providing some idea as to the nature of any difficulties a person may have, and the problems s/he may face, they can also be misleading and limit expectations. How individuals choose to react and respond to their experience differs from person to person. The only thing all people have in common is they are all different and, therefore, bring different qualities to everything they do. There are many individuals who respond by overcoming their adversity and becoming role models for others who, despite protective legislation and equal opportunities promotion, continue to have similar experiences.

Gender, Sex and Sexual Orientation

There are many people who think that, with the changes brought about by sex discrimination and equal pay legislation, there is now equality between the sexes and discrimination on the grounds of sex is very rare, or even nonexistent. However, many women are still in low paid jobs and are likely to earn less than men for similar work. They also continue to experience the 'glass ceiling' (when it looks as if there are opportunities to go higher but there is some barrier preventing this) and so are less likely to occupy positions of authority. Efforts have mainly focused on achieving equality based on entry into paid employment, with the result that women's family responsibilities remain unchanged. Equally, many men struggle with changing expectations of what makes a 'man', an issue which frequently, but not only, manifests when they can no longer be the main 'breadwinner'. Society's support of media's promotion of macho attitudes and role models means violence continues to be seen as acceptable, especially for males.

Also, the belief that the Sex Discrimination Act meant the end of sex discrimination is probably rooted in a narrow definition of sex and the acceptance that being anything other than heterosexual is wrong or abnormal. This is because the legislation largely applies to gender rather than sex, and does not protect people from discrimination on the grounds of their sexual orientation or sexual preference.

As with other areas of equal opportunities work, it is helpful to have an understanding of the terms that are used. There is a difference between sex and gender; in this context, sex is usually taken to refer to the biological female or male. Gender is the more social or cultural state of being female or male; this is thought to be learned, mainly through socialisation. There are also several other important terms relating to this aspect of equal opportunities work:

- sexual orientation – sometimes referred to as sexuality and usually taken to mean a person's sexual preference in respect of attraction to another

- bi-sexual – sexually attracted to both women and men

- heterosexual – sexually attracted to the opposite sex

- homosexual – sexually attracted to others of one's own sex. Currently in popular speech, 'lesbian' is used for sexual relationships between females and 'gay' refers to sexual relationships between males. While many people think the term 'queer' is politically incorrect, be aware some homosexuals may prefer this term as they feel 'gay' or 'lesbian' is not an appropriate 'label' for them

- transsexual – a person identified as one sex at birth (usually based on visible sex characteristics) but later discovered to have the physical sex characteristics of the opposite sex. This often manifests itself by having emotional and psychological feelings considered to be more appropriate to the opposite sex. Medical investigation often reveals internal, physical characteristics that match more to the sex the person feels her/himself to be, rather than what her/his visible characteristics lead them to be identified as. Transsexuals may or may not choose to undergo surgery to align how they feel themselves to be with their physical characteristics

- transvestite – a person, typically a man, who derives pleasure from dressing in clothes considered appropriate to the opposite sex; transvestites are not usually homosexuals

- sexism - the belief that there are characteristics, abilities or qualities specific to each sex and as some of these are valued more than others, one sex is superior to another (historically the male sex has been considered to be superior)

Sexism is unique among forms of discrimination in that those who experience it do not belong to a minority group; women make up 51% of the UK population.

Most of what early years practitioners deal with in their everyday work are gender issues, that is ensuring girls and boys have equal access to the experiences and opportunities. They do this very successfully, for example, by not discouraging girls from playing football or with construction toys. However, an issue frequently overlooked is how to actively encourage children to participate in a full range of experiences and opportunities. It is one thing to have toys and activities available for children, but a different one to get them to partake of these. Many girls remain reluctant to try physical activities and play with toys considered by many to be for boys, for example, playing with cars, and would benefit from adults 'modelling' these to them.

Equally, most boys remain reluctant to be involved with dressing up and playing with dolls (with the exception of Action Man!). Boys are often supported in their choices by reinforcement from fathers who believe playing with toys considered to be appropriate for girls will encourage their sons to be something other than heterosexual males. This is often rooted in the confusion that seems to suggest if boys come to enjoy dressing up this may make them homosexual. While there may be a chance the child becomes a transvestite, few transvestites are homosexual. Equally, the argument that dresses and skirts are inappropriate for males needs to be questioned, otherwise the kilt will need to be reviewed as appropriate attire, an argument most Scots (among others) would take issue with. In a society that is truly diverse and accepting of others it should not matter if a child grows up to be homosexual, transsexual or heterosexual. However, this is likely to remain an issue for some time in a society where by the age of five boys place more value on being male than female.

This argument also applies to the idea that a child of a homosexual couple will probably grow up to be homosexual. There is no evidence for this and, in a truly diverse and accepting society, it should not matter if a child does grow up to be homosexual, or transsexual, or heterosexual; although it has to be recognised that until unconditional acceptance is arrived at by the majority of society such a child may encounter difficulties. Unconditional acceptance at the earliest age will go a long way to alleviate potential future challenges.

As with all equal opportunities work, it is the active encouragement to challenge the current norms and status quo, that leads to better practice and allows each individual to achieve her/his potential.

Age

Currently in the UK about 40% of the adult population (19 million people) are aged 50 and over. The proportion of older people is growing, partly because the post-war baby boom generation is now reaching and passing 50 years of age. Also, a general decrease in birth rate over the last few decades means there are fewer young people. These demographic changes mean, by 2020, it is anticipated the 50 plus age group will have increased by a further 3 million.

As with other areas of equal opportunities work, it is helpful to have an understanding of frequently used terms:

- ageism – the belief that there are characteristics, abilities or qualities specific to particular ages and, as some of these are valued more than others, generally youth is considered superior to age

Age discrimination occurs when people are denied access to employment and the provision of goods, facilities and services because of their age. This can happen to both old and young people although usually for different reasons, for example, young children not being allowed to dine in some restaurants (often deemed not to be 'family-friendly') is just as ageist as someone being denied access to a nightclub because they are over 30. It can be argued that generally, in capitalist societies, people who are not economically productive (usually children and old people) are seen as a burden and thus valued less and consequently shown less respect. However, there is evidence older people experience more ageism, given that most western cultures value and respect youth more than age. Nevertheless, it is important to remember sometimes different treatment on grounds of age can be justified, for example, it may be necessary to make special provisions for younger or older people to protect their safety and welfare.

Although, in common with other discriminatory practices, ageism affects a whole range of opportunities, at present it is widely regarded that the most significant and damaging aspect of age discrimination is ageism in the workplace. Currently, approximately 6 million people aged between 50 and state pension age are in employment (a rate of 69%) and this age group have fewer qualifications than those aged 25-49, partly because of the changing value put on qualifications.

It is not necessary to be 'ancient' to experience ageism in the workplace, some companies have a policy of not employing people over the age of 30, or 40, regardless of whether or not the individual is qualified, skilled, and/or experienced to do the relevant work. Additionally, some companies who may be forced to make redundancies often select workers on the basis of how near they are to retirement age. However, it is anticipated these attitudes will have to change as older people form a larger and larger proportion of the workforce.

It is ageism in the workplace that is the government's current focus and, in supporting the European Directive on Equal Treatment, a commitment was made to implementing age legislation by 2006. The Code of Practice on Age Diversity was introduced in 1999. However, like other forms of discrimination, legislation alone will not affect either specific issues, for example, employment levels of older people, or general attitudes. In respect of ageism, a change in perspective, particularly toward older people, is also necessary.

Physical disability including special and additional needs

There are well over 8.5 million people with disabilities in the UK, that is approximately one in seven of the population. Unfortunately, some people think disability is only about being in a wheelchair. This misconception may arise from the fact that, historically, the majority of disability related signs featured images of a wheelchair. The reality is somewhat different: permanent wheelchair users make up less than 5% of the population of people with disabilities. About 11% of all 16-24 year olds have a long-term disability or health problem, while between 50 and state pension age, this figure rises to 33%. Also, many adults of working age regard mental illness as their main disability (for information on mental health see appropriate section).

As with other areas of equal opportunities work it is helpful to have an understanding of frequently used terms:

- disability – a physical or mental condition that limits a person's movements, senses (hearing, sight) or activities

- language – the method of communication either spoken or written, consisting of the use of words in an agreed way

- congenital – a faulty gene leads to a disabling condition, for example, cystic fibrosis, sickle-cell anaemia, Huntington's chorea

- developmental – when the foetus is growing, for example, the effects of rubella (German measles), X-rays

- accident or illness

There are several definitions of disability and a good starting point for equal opportunities is the definition found in the Disability Discrimination Act 1995. This defines a disabled person as 'anyone with a physical or mental impairment which has a substantial and long term adverse effect upon her/his ability to carry out normal day-to-day activities'. Although not a perfect definition, it does allow issues such as mental health problems, cancer, AIDS, dyslexia, severe disfigurement and epilepsy to be included under the Act.

So, in early years work, the issue of disability can relate to:

- children being cared for or educated

- people doing the caring or educating

- parents, main carers or close family members of the children

- people in the wider community who have contact with the care/education establishment

It is not appropriate to consider, because none of the children cared for have disabilities, equal opportunities related to disability is something of no concern. It can be argued there is a greater need for awareness raising among people who do not have contact with those who have disabilities. Even where there is contact with people with disabilities, this alone does not reduce fear or misconceptions, there is still a need to promote active learning about different people among adults and children. Also, because all disabilities are not visible, it is inappropriate to assume, because nobody is complaining, the facilities and opportunities you currently provide are adequate.

Traditionally, treatment of people with disabilities entailed segregation and exclusion, because society extended the differences between disabled and able-bodied people beyond physical disability to all or most other capabilities, including cognitive (thinking) capability. In some contexts, for example, athletics, health care and social service support, some physically disabled people may be different from other people, but they are not different in other respects. People with disabilities face discrimination when denied access to the same kind of lifestyle able-bodied people take for granted. Also, many people with disabilities wish to live as independently as non-disabled people, but may need support to do so. The range of discrimination that can be faced by people with disabilities is demonstrated by the following basic needs identified by independent living campaigners. To help achieve independent living, there should be equality in the provision of:

- physical access to the environment/housing

- physical access to transport

- equipment enabling independence

- personal assistance enabling independence

- inclusive education and training

- adequate income

- equal opportunities in employment

- accessible information

- advocacy (an advocate is a spokesperson) – leading towards self-advocacy

- empowering counselling services

- appropriate, accessible care

From birth most people like to share their experiences and communication is a large part of how people relate to one another. While communication does involve facial expressions, gestures and body language, and it is wise to remember this, most people when they refer to language usually mean verbal talking and listening. Thus, having language difficulties usually refers to experiencing problems with verbal talking and listening. For some disabilities, for example, autism, blindness, brain damage affecting speech, deafness and dumbness, such difficulties can be more common; but the degree of difficulty, if any, will vary from person to person. Consequently, some people may use sign or symbol languages such as Bliss symbols, British Sign Language or Makaton.

As people are individuals, no two people will be affected by a disability in exactly the same way. It is worth remembering the person who will know most about a specific disability is the person with that disability or her/his parent/main carer. It is also useful to remember people with a disability have the same basic needs as all other people, then they have some additional needs.

Including children and adults of all abilities should be seen as a challenge for both society and individual early years settings, rather than a challenge for those who have the additional needs. This is often referred to as 'our problem not their problem'. Again, as with other areas of equal opportunities work, it is the active encouragement of challenging current norms and the status quo, which leads to better practice and allows each individual to achieve her/his potential.

Special educational needs or Additional learning needs

People with special educational needs have learning difficulties or disabilities which make it harder for them to learn than most other people of the same age. Consequently, these people may need extra or different help from that given to others of the same age. Such people may or may not have a physical disability. People do not have learning difficulties just because their first language is not English, but of course some of these people may have learning difficulties as well. It is also important to note 'giftedness', (a term applied to children who are highly academically or artistically gifted for their age) may also be considered to be a special need.

As with other areas of equal opportunities work, it is helpful to have an understanding of frequently used terms:

- behavioural difficulties - for example, hyperactivity, attention deficit disorder (ADD), attention deficit hyperactivity disorder (ADHD), anti-social behaviour

- disability - a physical or mental condition that limits a person's movements, senses (hearing, sight) or activities

- language - the method of communication either spoken or written, consisting of the use of words in an agreed way

- sensory impairment - visual or hearing problems

- special educational needs (SEN) - learning difficulties that make it harder for the individual to learn than most others of the same age, such that extra or different help is required

- specific learning difficulties (SLD) - usually confined to reading, writing and numeracy, for example, dyslexia

- speech or language difficulties - delayed language in children, articulation problems, stuttering

Many learning difficulties and disabilities are diagnosed during early childhood, however some do not appear until later. The difficulties do not usually go away when the individual reaches the end of full-time education. Learning difficulties and disabilities can happen in three main ways:

- congenital - a faulty gene leads to a disabling condition, for example, Downs syndrome

- developmental - when the foetus is growing, for example, the effects of rubella (German measles) often blindness and/or deafness

- accident or illness which may lead to damaging of the brain, for example, meningitis

Children and adults with special educational needs or additional learning needs may need extra help for a range of needs, for example, thinking and understanding, physical or sensory difficulties, emotional and behavioural difficulties, difficulties with speech and language, or relating to and behaving appropriately with other people. The term 'additional learning needs' is sometimes used instead of 'special educational needs' when the individual has left full-time education.

So, in early years work, the issue of special educational needs, like physical disability, can relate to:

- children being cared for or educated

- people doing the caring or educating

- parents, main carers or close family members of the children

- people in the wider community who have contact with the care/education establishment

Similarly, it is not appropriate to consider because none of the children cared for have special educational needs, equal opportunities related to SEN is something of no concern. It can be argued there is a greater need for awareness raising among people who do not have contact with those who have special educational needs. Even where there is contact with people with SEN, this alone does not reduce fear or misconceptions, there is still a need to promote active learning about different people among adults and children. Also, because not all special educational needs are obvious, it is inappropriate to assume, because nobody is complaining, the opportunities and experiences you currently provide are adequate.

Special educational needs or additional learning needs means an individual could have difficulties and need support, with:

- expressing themselves or understanding what others are saying; making friends or relating to others

- behaving appropriately

- organising themselves

- sensory or physical needs

- reading, writing, number work, or understanding information

From birth most people like to share their experiences and communication is a large part of how people relate to one another. While communication does involve facial expressions, gestures and body language, and it is wise to remember this, most people when they refer to language usually mean verbal talking and listening. Thus, having language difficulties usually refers to experiencing problems with verbal talking and listening. For some disabilities, for example, autism, blindness, brain damage affecting speech, deafness and dumbness, such difficulties can be more common; but the degree of difficulty, if any, will vary from person to person. Consequently, some people may use sign or symbol languages such as Bliss symbols, British Sign Language or Makaton.

As people are individuals, no two people will be affected by a special educational need in exactly the same way. It is useful to remember that like all people with a disability, people with special educational needs have the same basic needs as all other people, then they have some additional needs. Also remember, including children and adults of all educational abilities should be seen as a challenge for both society and individual early years settings, rather than a challenge for those who have the additional educational needs. This is often referred to as 'our problem not their problem'. As with other areas of equal opportunities work, it is the active encouragement of challenging current norms and the status quo, which leads to better practice and allows each individual to achieve her/his potential.

Mental health

Mental health problems are common, yet widely misunderstood. Approximately one in six adults suffers from mental health problems of varying severity, ranging from anxiety (a neurosis) to psychotic disorders such as schizophrenia. Many people who experience mental health problems feel stigmatised by other people's attitudes and there are still some discriminatory practices in the workplace.

Mental health problems fall into two broad groups, neurosis and psychosis:

- neurosis – usually relatively mild mental illness with no loss of external reality, for example, anxiety, depression, obsessive behaviour

- psychosis – usually severe mental disorders in which thought and emotions are impaired, with possible loss of external reality, for example, schizophrenia

The precise nature and impact of the different conditions varies significantly from person to person, rarely being static, changing, disappearing and re-appearing during a person's life. Also, rates of diagnosis of mental illness vary between groups; research usually indicates a high rate amongst women and some black and minority ethnic groups, particularly African-Caribbean men, and there is a higher prevalence among ex-prisoners and people who sleep rough.

There are many factors that influence the development of mental health problems, including socio-economic disadvantage (that is, combined problems resulting from issues that relate to both society and economics), neighbourhood violence and crime, unemployment, poor educational attainment, being a member of an ethnic minority group, and being a lone parent or teenage mother. Also, mental health problems often co-exist with other issues, for example, substance misuse (drugs, alcohol, solvents, etc.), homelessness, poor physical health and learning disabilities.

Once mental health problems develop, they often have a negative impact on a wide range of opportunities including employability, housing, household income, access to services and social networks. People experiencing mental health problems are less likely to:

- take part in leisure, arts and community activities

- have strong family networks - individuals with psychotic disorders are more than three times as likely to be separated or divorced, and more than twice as likely to be living on their own as those without psychotic disorders

- have someone to talk to about their problems compared to the general population

- be employed

- access everyday goods and basic services such as health and banking services

- be living in appropriate or private housing

All of these can impact on each other creating a cycle, for example, long-term unemployment is associated with worsening mental health; and low levels of social participation can affect a person's quality of life, increase her/his social isolation and thus compound her/his problems. Both the problems and the cycle contribute to social exclusion and severe economic deprivation.

It is also a common misconception that children are too young to experience mental health problems. This is largely based on the fact many adults view childhood as being carefree and a time of no responsibility. However, there are an increasing number of children diagnosed with psychological problems including depression. Many young children have to deal with responsibilities such as caring for a disabled parent (and consequently, if applicable, younger siblings), living with parents who are alcoholics or drug addicts, living with disabled siblings, abuse, bullying, etc. All of these can have an impact on mental health.

Race and Nationality

Race and nationality are not just related to skin colour, although many people make this mistake. Also, many people confuse race and nationality with creed, or cultural background and practices. Although it can be difficult to separate the issues, partly because there can be links between them, it is beneficial to try to do so as it helps clarify many of the issues that impact on equal opportunities practice. Therefore, it is advisable to read this section in conjunction with the section on creed and cultural background.

For at least the last 5000 years, Britain has been peopled by migrants and, so it can be argued, has always had a diverse society. From the Bronze Age onwards people travelled to northwest Europe and continue to do so to the present day, for example the current eastern European and African refugees. So, most people in Britain today are either immigrants or the descendants of immigrants. This means Britain has benefited from ethnic diversity throughout its history. Individuals and groups from other countries and cultures have greatly enriched life for all by their many contributions to industry and commerce, sport, music and the arts, science and literature.

As with other areas of equal opportunities work, it is helpful to have an understanding of frequently used terms:

- ethnic – relating to a group of people having a common national or cultural tradition; indicating origin by birth or descent, rather than by present nationality

- language – the method of communication either spoken or written, consisting of the use of words in an agreed way

- nationality – the status of belonging to a particular nation (which is a large number of people united by common descent, culture, language inhabiting a particular geographic area)

- race – each of the major divisions of humankind, having distinct physical characteristics; a nation or group of people regarded by themselves or others as having a distinct ethnic origin

- racism – the belief that there are characteristics, abilities or qualities specific to each race and as some of these are valued more than others, some races are superior to others. It is based on the false idea that some physical characteristics (for example, skin colour), or ethnic background make some people better than others

It is not appropriate to consider because all the children you care for are white and/or British, equal opportunities is something of no concern. It can be argued there is a greater need for awareness raising among people who do not have contact with others who are not white and/or are from other countries. It is useful to remember children as young as two years old notice differences in skin colour and between the ages of three and five they begin to attach positive and negative values to these differences. Thus, although adults may like to think young children are incapable of developing negative or discriminatory attitudes, this is not so.

On a very basic level, it can be that skin colour is the most visible difference of race and, as this is easy to remember, it can become the identification point of race issues. Many cultures make associations between characteristics and colours and have done so for many centuries. In western culture, people have long associated white with goodness and positiveness, and black with badness and negativeness. This becomes problematic when these associations become beliefs and people begin to value some characteristics more than others, creating a hierarchy. In western culture white came to be valued more than black. This was encouraged by religious teachings and probably also influenced by the fact that here the majority of people are Caucasian (white); people like to feel good about themselves and use all kinds of psychological measures to boost their self-esteem.

Although there is no validity for any colour being better than another, when such ideas have been handed down from generation to generation, they become ingrained in a society's consciousness. Consider the number of Hollywood films where the bad guy can be quickly identified because he wears black! If other, so-called negative, characteristics then begin to be associated with black, and so-called positive ones with white, the characteristics can become compounded and stereotypes are born. Ingrained ideas and attitudes can be difficult to change, but not impossible. It is demeaning to encourage people to believe they are not capable of change and progress.

It is important to remember in respect of equal opportunities work, black has a very specific meaning and does not just refer to people who are not white. 'Black' is usually used when referring to people of African origin or descent; so this includes Afro-Caribbean people. Be aware though, some people, often (but not exclusively) those of south Asian heritage, object to being encompassed within the term 'black', as they do not consider it to be an accurate term, given their skin colour is not black and, if reference has to be made to their ethnicity, prefer this to be in terms of nationality. Additionally, although people from the Indian sub-continent are sometimes referred to as black, this confuses them with people of African origin, so their nationality, or that of their forebears, is usually used, for example, Indian, Pakistani. Likewise, when referring to the ethnicity of people from the Far East, nationality is usually used, for example Chinese, Vietnamese.

Differences in race and nationality can also be shown by language. An example of language demonstrating national difference is dialect, such as Irish, Scottish, or Welsh. Although two of these countries are British, they each have their own specific languages too, which are spoken by an increasing number of people. However, for many people who are not British, English is not their first language and so they may experience communication problems. Remember, this is not an issue that necessarily relates to skin colour, many Europeans come to live in this country and do not necessarily speak English. Not speaking English is not a learning difficulty or special educational need, and should not be treated as such. However, it is regarded as a specific need. Developing skills in English as an additional language (EAL) takes time, developing basic interpersonal communication skills in English takes a child one to two years, with a further five to seven years needed to achieve 'cognitive academic language proficiency'.

However, race related prejudice and discrimination is more than just an issue of skin colour or language. Many people who are white experience racism; historically, Irish people would fall into this category and can still be the butt of offensive jokes and derogatory comments. More recently many of the eastern European refugees who are seeking asylum in Britain have been the victims of racism. There are also times when discrimination is largely related to skin colour. Many British citizens experience racism possibly because they are not white, although they may not be black either, for example, people from the Pacific Rim – Hong Kong, Singapore. So the discrimination may relate to their creed, or cultural background.

Be aware particular difficulties can be faced by people in mixed race relationships and their families. In the UK, a mixed race relationship is often a white and a non-white person together, but of course can be non-white partners of two different ethnic groups, for example, an Afro-Caribbean person and an Indo-Chinese person. Many white women and men say they experience prejudice and discrimination from having a non-white partner. This feeling can be magnified if the partner is black and the prejudice comes from both the black and white communities. Also, non-white women, with racially different partners, can face similar prejudice and discrimination. Again, this is magnified if it comes from more than one community and, for non-white women, can sometimes result in exclusion from their 'community of identity'. For non-white men, the situation is not too much different to that of non-white women, with the potential for strong disapproval from other non-white men.

Children of mixed race parentage often face identity problems in that they can feel as though they do not fully belong to the ethnic community of either parent. In some respects, these children may face more prejudice and discrimination than children who belong to a distinct group. This is especially so if society promotes one culture as being better than another, or emphasises it is only possible to belong to one culture at once. This puts people of mixed race parentage under extreme pressure to choose one or the other and reject not just part of their heritage, but also relations for whom they feel a great deal of love and affection.

It is necessary to help all children to develop a positive sense of identity, whatever their racial background or nationality. As multi-cultural education does not prevent discrimination or racism, all children need to be encouraged to actively participate in a wide range of experiences and opportunities. Both prejudice and discriminatory remarks from adults and children, should be challenged whether these are made in front of children, adults, or both. Children should also be encouraged to do this too.

For some people their sense of identity is strongly tied to their ethnic or racial background and/or nationality, that is, their 'inherited' identity. Other people can feel a conflict between inherited identity and what can be referred to as 'public' identity, that is, their chosen identity or one which they feel they have to adopt in order to be accepted. Be aware that helping people to integrate into a dominant or majority culture can be viewed as racist practice. It cannot be over-emphasised the individuality of each person should be acknowledged, valued, and respected.

Creed and Cultural practices

Many people confuse creed and cultural background or practices with nationality or race and separating them can be difficult. This is because different ethnic backgrounds have created different religions (or branch of a religion) and developed cultural practices considered appropriate to the circumstances in which people found themselves. Although it can be difficult to separate the issues, partly because there can be links between them, it is beneficial to try to do so as it helps clarify many of the issues that impact on equal opportunities practice. Therefore, it is advisable to read this section in conjunction with the section on race and nationality.

All the people who have come to Britain in the last 5000 years have brought many of their cultural practices with them. Thus, it is not unreasonable to say there have always been many different cultures in Britain. Also, there have always been different faiths and sects in Britain, including agnosticism (not believing in a god), although they may not always have been visible, or been awarded the same status. Historically, it was considered beneficial to the unity and, therefore, strength of a country, for one faith to dominate. The Romans were instrumental in making this happen in Britain when they 'imported' Christianity.

As with other areas of equal opportunities work, it is helpful to have an understanding of frequently used terms:

- culture – the customs, civilisations and achievements of a particular time or people; the collective and dominant belief system of a group of people living close enough to influence one another

- creed – a system of religious belief or a faith

- faith – a strong belief in a religion

- religion – the belief in a superhuman controlling power especially in a personal God or Gods entitled to obedience and worship

Today the faiths practiced in Britain include Buddhism, Christianity, Hinduism, Islam (Muslim), Judaism, Rastafarianism and Sikhism, among others. Within all these faiths are subgroups or denominations (an autonomous branch of a religion) which have slightly different ways of practising the faith. This may include:

- dietary codes, for example, particular foods that can/cannot be eaten; specific ways of preparation

- dress codes, for example, covering the head; wearing of jewellery

- hygiene routines, for example, bathing, hair care

Just because a person has been born into or identifies with a particular faith does not mean s/he is an actively practising member of that faith. Nor does it mean s/he will necessarily practise all the tenets (principles) of that particular faith. The only way of knowing this is to ask the person her/himself.

In any country where one religion dominates, this can lead to intolerance, and possible persecution, of those who practice other religions. The same can also apply when no faith is allowed, or is discouraged, such as in some Communist countries.

Culture is created by the behaviour of a group of people. It includes events that happen on a regular basis, from daily to yearly or beyond. For example, it is a practice in most western cultures to take an annual holiday. Cultural practices can stem from ethnic origins, nationality or religion and include traditions and customs, many of which interlink with each other. Not everyone who claims a particular cultural background will practise all the customs and traditions, but s/he will probably follow the majority of them. The ones not followed may relate more to a religion, associated with the culture, but which the individual does not follow.

A list of cultural practices would be endless, not only does each culture have its own customs and traditions, but cultures evolve all the time. So while some practices are very old and longstanding, others are relatively new. A good illustration of this is youth culture, the music preferred by today's teenagers is not the same as a few years ago, never mind when you were that age! However, the musical style often goes on to become part of the culture. An example of a more longstanding cultural practice is that of travellers moving from place to place on a regular basis, (for information on travellers people see appropriate section).

Clothes can be another cultural indicator and some cultures have a traditional dress which may be worn everyday or just on special occasions, including at national festivals or on a country's patron saint day. For example, many Indian women wear a sari everyday, while in most of Scotland the kilt is reserved for special occasions. It is also traditional in some cultures to wear a lot of jewellery, or style hair in a particular fashion. Tattoos or body decoration are other cultural practices.

Most countries, and some regions, have specific food or dishes with which they are associated, some of which will be reserved for festivals and special occasions. For example, mince pies although associated with Christmas in Britain, are not a universal Christmas tradition. Language can also be used to help identify different cultures. Dialects and slang are not only found in local environments, but are used by media (films, magazines and television programmes) which may be associated only with a particular culture. Indian culture has its own thriving film industry, affectionately known by many as Bollywood.

For children whose parents follow cultural practices other than western ones and wish their children to do likewise, life can be particularly difficult. A conflict can be created between the culture encouraged at home and that promoted elsewhere, especially if the child's peers are of a different cultural background. This is sometimes referred to as the conflict between 'inherited' identity and 'public' identity. However, be aware that helping people to integrate into a dominant or majority culture can be viewed as racist practice.

It is necessary to help all children to develop a positive sense of identity, whatever their creed or cultural background. As stated before, multi-cultural education does not prevent discrimination or racism, all children need to be encouraged to actively participate in a wide range of experiences and opportunities. Both prejudice and discriminatory remarks from adults and children should be challenged whether these are made in front of children, adults, or both. Children should also be encouraged to do this too.

For some people their sense of identity is strongly tied to their cultural background and/or faith. Other people may derive a stronger sense of identity from their ethnic or racial background and/or nationality. For most people their sense of identity is created from a mixture of all of these, but the dominant aspects vary from person to person. Thus again, it cannot be over-emphasised the individuality of each person should be acknowledged, valued, and respected.

Refugees

Refugees are people who are forced to flee from their home and country because of serious danger or fear of persecution. The fear of persecution may be for reasons of race, religion, nationality, membership of a particular social group or political opinion. Someone seeking refugee status in another country is called an asylum seeker and has to apply for official refugee status.

Most recently asylum seekers in Britain have come from the former Yugoslavia, Sri Lanka, Turkey, Somalia, Nigeria and Iraq. As can be seen, this indicates a variety of linguistic, cultural and religious backgrounds. English may or may not be spoken.

It is important to remember many refugees have usually left their homes in very distressing circumstances and will have traumatic memories of how they came to be in their present situation. They may have had to leave family members behind knowing they are still in danger or missing and yet have little or no contact with them for reassurance. Additionally, they have to familiarise themselves with living in a strange country, often in temporary accommodation, not knowing whether they will be allowed to remain in Britain. In these circumstances it is not unusual for children to regress in development and adults to experience stress.

Traveller communities and People who follow specific alternative lifestyles

A travelling lifestyle is followed by a number of communities, including English and Welsh gypsies, Irish and Scottish travellers, showmen (fairground people), circus people, bargees or boat dwellers and those who choose specific alternative lifestyles, for example, 'new age' travellers. Many of the groups generally find the term 'traveller' acceptable, but 'gypsy' is a term which only some of them find acceptable and often it is perceived as being negative. It is worth remembering Romany Gypsies and Irish Travellers are distinct ethnic groups and protected under Race Relations legislation. Some gypsies prefer to be referred to as Roma and they will often speak the Romany language.

With the exception of those who choose specific alternative lifestyles, all the communities have a long tradition of a travelling lifestyle, although the background and customs vary from group to group. Showmen, circus people and bargees have their own traditional occupations and history of planned movement. In the last twenty years, some people have specifically chosen alternative lifestyles and become travellers for a variety of reasons. More recently still, many Roma people from central and eastern Europe have sought political asylum in Britain.

Many travellers live in conventional housing and may no longer travel, though they consider themselves to be ethnically and culturally travellers. Some live on caravan sites (either local authority or privately owned) or on their own plot of land. A serious lack of suitable accommodation means about 20% of the traveller population has no secure place to stay and so move between unauthorised encampments. Obviously, in such circumstances, access to basic services, for example health and education, is difficult and sometimes impossible.

There a very few traditional boat dwelling families still living on the inland waterway network in Britain and very little is known about the number of bargee children.

Travelling patterns vary and sometimes are seasonal:

Showmen - the travelling season starts about the beginning of March and fairs usually move every week or two packing up on Sunday, travelling part of Monday and setting up ready to open again on Wednesday. Although families sometimes live in touring caravans it is more usual to find them in large living-wagons (like mobile homes) which have several spacious rooms and a fully equipped bathroom. At the end of the season (about the beginning of November), many families return to winter quarters, although some go abroad to work for the winter. While equipment is repaired and stored, some adults take winter jobs. This is also a time for annual holidays and celebrations.

Circus families – have very similar living accommodation and seasonal travelling patterns to Showmen, although circuses usually move every week and some do not have a permanent winter base. Children who travel with circuses may be performers, or the children of performers or other circus staff, and may come from any country. As the circus usually only spends one week in each place, the children go to a new school every four or five days.

Gypsy and Irish Traveller families – do not necessarily plan travel in advance. They often travel for family events, for example, weddings or funerals, extended visits to relatives, to visit traditional horse fairs and similar celebrations, or when looking for work. As a result of the combined effects of prejudice from the settled community, mobility, low literacy levels and lack of school experience on the part of some of the parents, this group in particular can find it difficult to access the education system.

Roma families – eastern European Roma people share a common history and culture and some elements of a common language with British Romany Gypsies. Although accommodation in their home countries varies, it is often conventional housing or apartments. Any Roma family seeking political asylum in Britain, like other refugees, will be placed in temporary accommodation.

People choosing specific alternative lifestyles – do not necessarily have a travelling pattern and some travel only rarely (no more than non-travelling people). Accommodation covers a wide range from caravans or converted buses to tents or boats. Many children have been born into these communities and know no other lifestyle.

Many traditional traveller families are very protective of their children and dislike exposing them to environments outside the family circle; they can find it difficult to trust their children to the care of non-travellers. It is not uncommon among traditional travellers for girls and boys to be brought up to change in private and be deeply embarrassed by communal changing. Also, some normally never remove jewellery. Discriminatory problems can also be compounded, particularly among traditional traveller families, by the stigma attached to adults who have few or no literacy skills.

Lone parents

Lone parenthood is not as recent a phenomenon as some people would like to believe. Western culture values families for the security and stability they can bring to society. Convention, stemming from the dominance and controlling power of religion, declared families had to be created by couples. There was strong disapproval of anyone who strayed from this norm. Society was structured to only support children through marriage and eventually there was financial help available for widows. For many people there is still a stigma attached to lone parenthood. Besides the historical element, some of the stigma stems from the view that all lone parents are poorly educated, unskilled, young women who rely on social security benefits. Not surprisingly, this is not a wholly accurate picture.

There are about 1.7 million lone parent families in the United Kingdom. Most lone parents are women in the 25-40 age group and have become so through separation or divorce. This may not have been their choice, but have come about by their partner's insistence or as a result of their partner's behaviour, for example incidents of violence, or a partner who is serving a prison sentence. Separation and divorce are not the only reasons for lone parenthood. Some people choose not to marry yet still have children, or choose to foster or adopt children despite being single. Also, some people may have become single parents through being widowed. Additionally, about 10% of lone parent families are headed by fathers.

Lone parents can experience financial hardship, even though they may work. It is not uncommon for lone parents to be in full-time work, particularly when they have school-aged children. For those who have to rely on benefits this is usually through necessity not choice. However, for many lone parents it is not financial insecurity that is the major issue. For some lone parents who experienced violence or abuse from a partner, the lack of physical threat and peace of mind brought about by separation and/or divorce outweighs any financial restrictions. Also, while some people may find the sole responsibility of decision-making challenging, others appreciate the opportunity to make decisions, free from the influence of a partner.

Raising children is always challenging and this is additionally so when a parent has sole responsibility for the children, as is the case for most lone parents. One of the most stressful tasks is attempting to be both mother and father and the role of the opposite gendered parent may prove particularly difficult. Few women know how to be fathers and the mysteries of motherhood elude many single fathers! In these circumstances single parents frequently compensate for what they think the child is missing, although this may not in fact be amiss. Some divorced or separated parents do manage to share child-rearing with ex-partners, but others, for a variety of reasons, prefer to discourage access between their children and ex-partners. This lack of contact may have adverse effects on the children even though it may be done with the best of intentions.

Although lone parent families are far more common today, children from these families can still feel different, especially if the nuclear family is promoted as the norm. As well as the possibility of feeling rejected and/or abandoned, they may also be affected by not experiencing the role modelling influence of their 'absent' parent. The latter is particularly pertinent to teenagers and some people think the social development of boys is adversely affected if they do not have a strong, close male influence, preferably a father. Children of widows or widowers have, additionally, to deal with bereavement. Also, children of mixed race relationships may have to deal with the prejudice of having a parent who is not the same colour as themselves.

Extended families

Conventionally, the extended family has been described as beyond the nuclear family. With changing social patterns and greater numbers of people divorcing, re-marrying, choosing to co-habit or remain single, the description of the extended family has changed. Unfortunately, in some respects the definition has become more complicated, as different types of family have been accommodated. However, the positive side of this means there are fewer specific 'labels' that can be attached to individuals and families and this should lead to less discrimination.

The nuclear family is generally taken to be parents (one or both) and children who live together, separately from other relatives; this may be some distance from other family members, such as grandparents and aunts and uncles. Thus traditionally, the extended family incorporated grandparents, aunts, uncles and cousins who either lived with, or in very close proximity to, the nuclear family. Some cultural groups continue to value and maintain this type of extended family.

In recent years, one of the effects of separation, divorce, and remarriage is many families have become 're-ordered'. While many children grow up in a single-parent household having no contact with the parent with whom they do not live, many other children live in two households, moving from one to the other usually at the weekend and holiday time. If parents have remarried or choose to co-habit with another partner this can mean the extended family includes one or more stepparents, half-sisters and half-brothers and/or stepsisters and brothers or these in any combination. Single, unmarried parents marrying for the first time can also provide children with an immediate stepfamily. Some children will have half-sisters and half-brothers by virtue of the fact their parents choose to have children by several different partners. The different types of extended family mean children may have more than two sets of grandparents. Additionally, some children may live with specific extended family members, for example, grandparents on a permanent basis.

These differences can put great strain on particularly young children, especially if the nuclear family is promoted as the norm. The number of people with whom relationships have to be formed can be very challenging and the web of relationships very confusing. Also, the size of the extended family may mean there are financial difficulties. It is not unusual for fathers, in particular, to have to financially support children from a previous marriage or relationship at the same time as those in their current marriage or relationship. This can leave the children of the second or subsequent relationship feeling disadvantaged and in some cases second wives have had to work to help maintain the children from the first marriage.

People with caring responsibilities

People with caring responsibilities are those who care, unpaid, for older, often aged, dependents, or partners/family members who are frail, have disabilities, or terminal illness. It includes foster families as well as people who have responsibility for their grandchildren although they may not be official foster parents, and children who find themselves the main carer for a parent with a disability or illness. It is not unknown for some children who are classified as main carers to be below secondary school age and as well as their parent, they may be responsible for younger siblings. There are 5.7 million people in the UK who care for a relative, partner or friend, or for a child with a disability.

Adults who are carers can find their life becomes consumed by their caring responsibilities. Many say they do not have a life of their own because of the daily care routine of the person who is dependent on them. This can be 24 hours if their dependent does not have a sense of responsibility and awareness of danger and, so possibly, may be a danger to her/himself. Naturally, this is exhausting and carers frequently find themselves with no time for activities most people take for granted, for example, going to the hairdressers. They can also find their privacy curtailed, as some dependents cannot be left alone and this can be extremely stressful. Not surprisingly, many carers experience emotional or psychological illness and this can impact upon their ability to care.

Children who are carers usually miss out on the activities most people assume are a normal part of childhood. Having to complete domestic duties such as shopping and laundry, as well as possibly helping their parent with bathing and other intimate, personal hygiene tasks, leaves little time for their own interests or hobbies. Performing such responsible tasks also means the child tends to mature very quickly and they may have an awareness of some things which still elude many adults. School attendance and work can also suffer.

Many carers benefit from respite care, which allows them to retain some sense of psychological wellbeing. Respite care is when the carer can have some time to her/himself because someone else cares for their dependent. This may only amount to a couple of hours a month as some local authorities and health authorities find it difficult to provide sufficient, appropriate services and facilities. While some families are able to organise some respite care amongst themselves, by other family members 'taking a turn', this is not possible where the carer is an only child or has few other close family relations.

For carers of dependents who are terminally ill, respite care can sometimes be offered for longer periods of time, often in a hospice. It should not be assumed where this happens, the people involved do not wish to maintain daily contact and the carer not be involved in the dependent's care. However, this can create different problems and, therefore stress, if the carer does not have access to transport or the financial resources to fund visits.

Children who are carers rarely benefit from respite care. Sometimes few, if any, people outside the immediate family know of the responsibilities carried by these children. In some cases, the situation can come to light when a child's non-attendance at school is investigated. However, many children who are carers understandably have a great sense of loyalty to the family and can be very good at hiding the situation from adults in authority, no matter how concerned or caring those adults. Some of these children, and their parents, fear they will be taken into local authority care if the true extent of the situation is revealed.

Although most people who care for dependents do so in their own home, this does not have to be the case. Even if physical care is done by professional carers in a home or hospice, the responsibility of decisions regarding the dependent and their care may remain and this can be stressful. Many people do not like committing their loved ones to institutional care and, along with a sense of failure, feel guilt. This can be the case even when they know the dependent will get better care than they may be able to provide. Also maintaining contact with dependents in homes/hospices may be difficult without access to transport or sufficient financial resources.

Teenage parents

Teenage pregnancy rates in England are high by European standards - one in every 14 babies born in England is to a teenage mother. Research indicates the risk of teenage parenthood is greatest for those from the poorest backgrounds, and those who truant, are excluded from school or leave with low educational attainment.

Most of what is written about teenage parenthood focuses on teenage mothers, teenage fathers tend to be ignored, yet they do exist. However, it should not be assumed the father of a teenage mother's child is also a teenager although they may still be young. Some information of teenage fathers can be found in research on young offenders. Many male young offenders are fathers and feel very strongly that they would like a stronger relationship with their child/ren. This is particularly true if a young father comes from a background where he did not have a close relationship with his own father.

Pregnancy before the legal age of majority is not new and historically in western culture, working class young mothers would have ended up in the workhouse, while those from the upper classes may have been thrown out of home or been committed to a mental asylum. Over time, as social attitudes changed, young, particularly unmarried, mothers were encouraged to give up their babies for adoption immediately after the birth. Further changes in attitude brought about by the women's liberation movement, along with changes in social welfare in the 1970's, made it more acceptable for women to keep and raise the children by themselves.

Nevertheless, modern society still tends to disapprove of pregnancy in young girls and particularly where this occurs before the official school leaving age. It is to this group that teenage parenthood and teenage pregnancy usually refers. There is still stigma attached to being a teenage parent, some of which will be generated by the fact that most will be single parents. This is largely because marriage under the age of eighteen is legal only with parental consent and parents of teenage children may not be prepared to do this. This of course assumes marriage would be the most appropriate action, which is not necessarily the case. It is difficult to assess how much of the stigma is related to age, how much to lone parenthood and how much to the combination, creating a double disadvantage (for more information on lone parenthood see appropriate section).

Undoubtedly, raising children can be challenging and many think it is additionally challenging for teenagers, who are often considered to lack maturity. Teenagers usually also lack the considerable financial resources needed to raise a child, thus there is a greater chance these families will find themselves living in poverty (for more information on low income families see appropriate section). Hence much of the government's focus regarding teenage parenthood is to reduce the number of school age girls who become pregnant. However, like all new parents, teenage parents (mothers and fathers) need help and support with both practical child-rearing and the psychological changes brought about by the responsibility of being a parent.

Today, many teenage mothers initially live with their own parent(s), who help with the care and raising of the baby, although it is still not unknown in some circumstances for pregnant girls to be thrown out of home. Some strictly religious families still consider it a disgrace for children to be born out of wedlock and choose to disown their pregnant daughters. Local education authorities have resources to provide education during the pregnancy and after the birth and this is usually encouraged. Local authorities can also provide assistance with accommodation, but this more likely to be of the bed and breakfast variety rather than a house or flat.

Unless living with the mother, teenage fathers may have little contact with their children. Remember though, this may not be the choice of the father; for a variety of reasons, mothers may discourage and even make it difficult for a child's father to have access to the child.

Families of prisoners/ex-offenders

Undoubtedly there is a stigma to being a criminal. This is part of society's reason for having a criminal justice system – to control the behaviour of its members by disapproving of and so punishing, some acts to such an extent people are persuaded not to act in that manner. Often the magnitude of the disapproval relates to the seriousness of the crime, for example, murder, rape or child abuse rate more disapproval than theft, or parking offences. Having completed a sentence, the stigma does not necessarily go away; in fact the use of the term ex-offender ensures an individual is reminded of her/his actions.

It is important not to assume all prisoners and ex-offenders are men, although it has to be acknowledged women, for a variety of reasons, are less likely to receive prison sentences. Equally, it may be the offender or ex-offender in the family is a child, much as we may not like to think of young children committing crimes. An ex-offender has completed their sentence, but this will not necessarily have been a prison sentence. Many of the issues encountered by the families of prisoners or ex-offenders can also be experienced by families of people who are on remand or awaiting trial.

Like there is a stigma attached to being a criminal, there can be a stigma attached to being part of the family of a prisoner or ex-offender. Rather than treat all family members as individuals, there is a tendency for people to assume traits (characteristics) run in families. Thus, it may be assumed because a person's father or elder brother is, or has been, in prison, other family members are bound to follow the same course. This can have a major impact on children in particular, who eventually may decide, as this is expected of them, they will fulfil the prophecy.

Families of prisoners who wish to maintain contact with them during their sentence may find this difficult, as sentences are not often served at local prisons. Also visiting does tend to be limited, possibly only a few hours a month. This can lead to the breakdown of families, creating lone parents, even if only temporarily, and is usually disruptive of relationships between children and parent(s). It may be if a mother is serving a prison sentence that her children are taken into the care of social services. (For information on lone parents see appropriate section.)

Families of prisoners and ex-offenders may experience financial hardship. Ex-offenders can find it difficult to gain employment; and if previously an offender was employed, their income will stop when they go to prison. So it may be necessary to rely on social security benefits or, if possible, other adults in the family to seek employment.

Low income families - poverty, unemployment

Many people who live in poverty belong to groups which experience discrimination and prejudice. Poverty is usually defined as the lack of resources to obtain the type of diet, participate in the activities, and have living conditions and amenities which are customary or widely encouraged in society. Thus poverty can differ from country to country and from time to time. Research indicates people with children are at higher risk of experiencing poverty than those without children, with single parents being particularly vulnerable. Also at higher risk are people with disabilities, people from ethnic minority groups and the elderly.

There are many reasons for poverty, for example, unemployment, chronic illness, disability, low income, lack of educational opportunities, single parenthood. Additionally, many of these reasons combine together making it very difficult to break the poverty cycle; for example, a person who has experienced a poor education resulting in few, if any, qualifications may also experience poorly paid employment and periods of unemployment.

Obviously, poverty has an impact on health and well being, with more illness and accidents being experienced by people categorised as belonging to the lower two social classes. Also, children with parents in professional/managerial positions are more likely to be higher up the educational development distribution (a way of linking educational development to environmental factors), than those whose parents are considered partly or unskilled in job terms, or who have lower educational attainment themselves. Although insufficient income is central to poverty, it is not just about shortage of money; it is about how people are treated and how they regard themselves.

Poverty encroaches on all aspects of daily life and while the most obvious impact is having to do without things, for example, new clothes, trips or holidays, it can also mean being denied access to decent housing, good health, education, a social life and a sense of self esteem which most people in western society take for granted. Thus, consequences of poverty include powerlessness, exclusion and loss of dignity. Also, some researchers have also suggested children from low income families learn to scale down their hopes and aspirations as a result of diminished expectations of what their parents can afford, that is they 'learn to be poor'. For this reason 'social exclusion' is a term frequently used instead of poverty, and equal access to opportunities and experiences apply to those at risk from social exclusion as much as to the more conventional sex, race and disability discriminations.

Geographic disadvantage – rural, and pocketed deprivation

People who live in urban areas with a reasonable choice of services and reach to them through good transportation, often take such things for granted and assume the situation is the same for all. However, people who live in rural areas frequently experience social isolation because of poor or non-existent public transport, this can make it difficult to get to work and access key services such as education and healthcare. Even in seemly wealthy urban areas there can be pockets of deprivation – areas where facilities and services are limited, or the people who live there do not have the financial resources to access such services.

Wherever transportation is a problem through timing or location of services, people can find it more difficult to get and keep jobs, get to school, college, or healthcare, and purchase fresh food. For example, every year, 1.4 million people miss, turn down or choose not to seek medical help because of transport problems; and 40% of jobseekers say problems with transport are a key barrier to getting work. Also, people who live in rural areas do not have access to the same levels of social and recreational provision as those who live in towns and cities, this can be particularly difficult for young people.

While people in rural communities may experience the benefits associated with living in fairly cohesive communities, an aspect of such communities frequently ignored is what has been termed 'social policing'. In small communities where following tradition, or convention, is strong, the pressure to conform to acceptable norms can be particularly heavy and disapproval (one aspect of social policing) can mean choices are restricted. Also, some opportunities may never be considered as they fall outside what the community deem acceptable. Additionally, there can be a feeling of limited privacy - everyone knows every other person's business, this may make it difficult for some people to talk about their feelings.

Homelessness

The common image of homelessness is of people sleeping rough on the streets. This is not an experience of choice for many homeless people, although it would not be appropriate to think homelessness can be solved by providing all homeless people with accommodation. Some older homeless people in particular, claim this is their preferred lifestyle and resist attempts to find them accommodation. Often this may be the case if the accommodation is to be a residential home.

Not all people who are homeless sleep rough, as the category includes people who need temporary accommodation. People who live in hostels, women and their children who need the services of refuges and families who live in bed and breakfast accommodation are often considered to be homeless. Asylum seekers are not usually considered to be homeless. Asylum seekers are usually considered to be displaced rather than homeless.

People may find themselves homeless for a variety of reasons and this is not a problem just associated with urban areas; although many people move to the towns and cities as they feel this is where there will be more opportunities. Factors contributing to homelessness include debt and consequent inability to pay mortgage or rent; unemployment, especially where accommodation is 'tied' to the job; violence or abuse from a partner or, in the case of children, parents; inadequate social care system - children or adults. Some of the adults may have mental health problems, or additional learning needs and have found it too difficult to manage in the community without support. Some young people who leave local authority care at the age of sixteen can eventually find themselves homeless if too little time was given to preparing them to live independently.

Many of the homeless people on the streets are single and their experience may involve begging because of difficulty in accessing social security benefits, through not having an address. Unfortunately, many feel they have no alternative but to turn to crime to support themselves. Some single homeless people turn to alcohol or drugs, although for others this may have been a contributory factor in them becoming homeless. Many young children who run away from home to escape abuse often find themselves involved in prostitution (boys as well as girls).

It is not unusual to find that these people do not stay in one place for any length of time, although others can eventually establish a 'patch' and routine for themselves. Poor diet and exposure to bad weather often eventually lead to ill health. Undoubtedly, the stigma attached to being homeless contributes to people being reluctant to access health and social services. Also, previous poor experiences of services where an individual has been left feeling unheard or misunderstood and unaccepted rather than supported adds to this reluctance.

Living in hostels or bed and breakfast accommodation usually means there is limited, if any, access to basic cooking and laundry facilities. There can also be a lack of privacy and space, a particular difficulty where children are concerned. Children who do have to live in temporary accommodation may find their education is disrupted and friendships are put under strain, through lack of regular contact or simply because they cannot have friends around to play. Additionally, the family may have to exist on social security benefits as it is difficult to find employment without a permanent address. For people who are in work, the immense stress and strain of homelessness means they may find themselves having to give up work unless they have an exceptionally understanding employer.

The psychological impact of being homeless is enormous. The lack of security caused by being deprived of permanent shelter, one of the fundamental necessities of life, impacts on everything else in a individual's life. Consequently, people who are homeless frequently experience multiple disadvantage.

Multiple disadvantage

Some of the categories detailed in this section overlap or interlink and so people may find themselves experiencing multiple disadvantage. Quite simply, this is experiencing more than one disadvantage at any one time. Therefore, people who experience multiple disadvantage can find any problems they have appear to be compounded and this can be extremely demoralising. However, multiple disadvantage is not additive, that is, just one problem on top of another. How one form of disadvantage is experienced is influenced by, and influences, how another form is experienced. More than one disadvantage should not be regarded as a further disadvantage, but as a different disadvantage.

Thus, it should not automatically be assumed all the possible problems associated with any one individual circumstance will all come together in multiple disadvantage. The combination of issues will vary from person to person and situation to situation and may even vary from time to time. This makes multiple disadvantage difficult to define specifically and so possible cases have to be defined and treated individually. However, this is precisely what equal opportunities practice is about, appreciating, as people are individuals, their reactions and responses to circumstances will be different. Nevertheless, in common with all the other issues discussed, any problems associated with multiple disadvantage need to be dealt with sensitively.

Reflection

Do I personally identify with any of the groups mentioned?

-
-
-

What do I feel about this identification?

-
-
-

Am I aware of anyone else who has had any of these experiences?

-
-
-

How do I actively support people who experience prejudice, discrimination, harassment and/or stereotyping?

-
-
-

Legislation

This section outlines some of the key legislation underpinning equal opportunities work. It is not a comprehensive statement of the various pieces of legislation.

Human Rights Act 1998

This came into full force in the UK from 2nd October 2000. It gives further effect to fundamental rights and freedoms available for the previous 50 years, in the European Convention on Human Rights (ECHR), by incorporating rights under the Convention into domestic law. It is a law that affects all other laws, as whenever the government proposes a new law in parliament under the Human Rights Act, it has to make a statement about how the new law fits in with the Convention rights. Also UK courts and tribunals have to interpret domestic law, as far as possible, in accordance with Convention rights.

The rights (and limitations) included in the Act can be thought of as a set of basic values. It is hoped that respect for these rights can help change the way people think and behave, and create an atmosphere in which decisions and policies can be discussed and understood. A further hope is that by respecting the values enshrined in the Act, this will improve tolerance and thus the quality of life will be improved for all.

The Human Rights Act mainly affects the behaviour of public authorities (for example, government, civil servants, local authorities, health authorities) and agencies (for example, police, courts, private companies carrying out public functions). It ensures that those in authority have to check that they do not neglect or ignore your rights even when they believe they are doing so for good reason. They have to try to strike a balance and consider how to cause the least possible harm to individuals.

The Act should also encourage transparency and openness.

The 16 basic rights in the Human Rights Act are all taken from the European Convention on Human Rights. As well as affecting matters of life and death, like freedom from torture and killing, they also affect your rights in everyday life, for example, what you can say and do, your beliefs, your right to a fair trial. The list that follows briefly outlines the 16 rights:

Right to life - you have the right to have your life protected by law, although there are certain limited exceptions when it is acceptable for the State to take away someone's life, for example, a police officer acting justifiably in self-defence.

Prohibition of torture - you have the right not to be tortured or subjected to treatment/punishment which is inhuman or degrading.

Prohibition of slavery and forced labour - you have the right not to be treated as a slave or forced to perform certain kinds of labour.

Right to liberty and security - you have the right not to be deprived of your liberty (arrested/detained) except in certain limited cases and where this is justified by a clear legal procedure, for example, suspicion/conviction of committing a crime.

Right to a fair trial - you have the right to a fair and public hearing within a reasonable period of time. This is applicable to both criminal charges against you and civil rights/obligations cases. Hearings must be by a legally established, independent, impartial tribunal. The public can be excluded from the hearing (but not the judgement) if it is necessary to protect national security or public order. For criminal charges you are presumed innocent until proved guilty according to law and have certain guaranteed rights to defend yourself.

No punishment without law - you normally have the right not to be found guilty of any offence arising out of actions which at the time committed were not criminal. You are protected against later increases in the possible sentence for offences.

The rights in the next three articles may be limited where it is necessary to achieve an important objective, for example, protecting public health or safety, preventing crime, protecting the rights of others.

Right to respect for private and family life - you have the right to respect for your private and family life, your home and correspondence. This right can only be restricted in specified circumstances.

Freedom of thought, conscience and religion - you are free to hold a broad range of views, beliefs and thoughts, along with religious faith. Limitations are permitted only in specified circumstances.

Freedom of expression - you have the right to hold opinions and express your views (including those that are unpopular or disturbing) on your own and in a group. This right can only be restricted in specified circumstances.

Freedom of assembly and association - you have the right to assemble with other people in a peaceful way. You also have the right to associate with other people, which can include the right to form a trade union. These rights may be restricted only in specified circumstances.

Right to marry - you have the right to marry and start a family. National law governs how and at what age this can happen.

Prohibition of discrimination - in applying the rights of the Convention, you have the right not to be treated differently because of your race, religion, sex, political views or any other status, unless this can be justified objectively. Everyone has equal access to the rights of the Convention, regardless of status.

Protection of property - you have the right to the peaceful enjoyment of your possessions. Public authorities cannot usually interfere with things you own or the way you use them except in specified limited circumstances.

Right to education - you have the right not to be denied access to the educational system.

Right to free elections - elections for members of the legislative body (Parliament) must be free and fair, taking place by secret ballot. There may be qualifications imposed on voting eligibility, for example, minimum age.

Abolition of the death penalty - these provisions abolish the death penalty. There can be limited exceptions in times of war, but only in accordance with clearly specified laws.

As an individual you cannot use the Human Rights Act directly to sue or be sued for breaking the Convention rights. However, you can bring claims against public authorities for breaches of Convention rights. Now that all laws have to be given a meaning and effect that is as close as possible to the Convention rights, it is much easier to insist on your rights as this will be written in national law. It is also easier to bring them to the attention of people who you think are ignoring them.

As with any rights there are also responsibilities. Under the Human Rights Act you do not have unlimited rights; this helps to ensure that everyone is treated fairly. Most of the rights in the Act have boundaries to prevent them from both unfairly affecting the rights of others and overriding the rights of the wider community, for example, restricting someone's right to liberty if they have committed a crime. There is also the idea of 'proportionality', that is your rights can only be interfered with in so far as it is necessary to achieve a specific purpose set out in the Convention. An example of this would be the right to assembly and to meet with others, so a blanket ban on demonstrations or marches because of fears for public safety would be inappropriate; measures must be appropriate to safeguard against reasonably anticipated risks to others without denying the right to assemble.

Further information on the Human Rights Act is available from the Human Rights Unit at the Home Office (contact details can be found in the Appendix).

Sex Discrimination Act 1975 and 1986

This legislation applies to all men, women and children in England, Wales and Scotland. Northern Ireland has its own equivalent legislation - Sex Discrimination Act (Northern Ireland) Order 1976 (amended 1988). It prohibits direct and indirect sex discrimination against individuals in areas of employment, education, and the provision of goods, facilities, services and in the disposal or management of premises. It also prohibits discrimination in employment against married people, however, it is not unlawful to discriminate against someone because they are not married. The legislation does not protect people from discrimination on the grounds of their sexual orientation or sexual preference, however the Sex Discrimination (Gender Reassignment) Regulations 1999 explain the special provisions about discrimination on the grounds of gender reassignment in the employment field.

Victimisation because someone has tried to exercise their rights under the Sex Discrimination Act is prohibited. Discriminatory advertisements are unlawful, but only the Equal Opportunities Commission can take action against advertisers.

The main exceptions to the Act are:

- when a charity is providing a benefit to one sex only, in accordance with its charitable instrument

- when people are competing in a sport in which the average woman is at disadvantage to the average man because of physical strength, stamina or physique

- in insurance where the discrimination reasonably relates to actuarial or other data

Direct sex discrimination

This occurs when someone is treated less favourably than someone of the opposite sex in comparable circumstances because of her or his sex. Examples of direct sex discrimination include sexual harassment or treating a woman adversely because she is pregnant.

Indirect sex discrimination

This occurs when a condition or practice is applied to both sexes, but the majority of one sex is not able to comply with it and it cannot be justified (regardless of sex) to apply that condition/practice, so a person is disadvantaged as a result. Examples of indirect sex discrimination include an unnecessary height requirement or a requirement to work full-time.

Discrimination in employment

In general it is unlawful to discriminate on the grounds of sex or marriage in recruitment and selection, treatment at work, or dismissal. However, if one of the defined genuine occupational requirements applies, sex discrimination in recruitment will be lawful. Examples of genuine occupational requirement are: if a role in a play needs to be played by a woman for authenticity, or the job needs to be done by a man to preserve decency and privacy.

Employees and potential employees have rights under the Sex Discrimination Act whatever their length of employment and whatever hours are worked. There are also special provisions preventing discrimination by people providing vocational training.

Discrimination in education

Co-educational schools, colleges and universities must not discriminate on the grounds of sex in the way they admit or treat pupils or students. The Sex Discrimination Act does not have specific directions in terms of different stages of education and undoubtedly in recent years there have been major changes in early years education including the recognition that it is sometimes difficult to separate education from childcare. Consequently, it is worth knowing how the Act applies to schools, in order to ensure equality of opportunity wherever a child accesses early years education. Many of these directions can also apply to out of school care facilities.

The Act states it is unlawful to discriminate on the grounds of sex in the following ways:

- refusing an application for admission
- applying different terms to girls and boys in an offer to admit them to the school
- refusing to allow one sex access to any benefits, facilities or services that are open to the other sex
- giving one sex different benefits, facilities or services from the other sex
- excluding them from the school
- subjecting them to any other form of detriment

An exception is made for admission to single-sex schools, but it should be remembered that the facilities in such establishments should not be inferior to those of others in the area.

Discrimination in the provision of goods, facilities, services and in the disposal or management of premises

Generally, it is unlawful to discriminate on the grounds of sex in the provision of goods, facilities, services and in the disposal or management of premises and there are few exceptions to this part of the Sex Discrimination Act. Exceptions include:

- discrimination by non-profit making voluntary bodies in restricting membership or providing benefits to one sex in accordance with their main object

- discrimination in provision of facilities/services to avoid serious embarrassment to users which would be caused by the presence of members of the opposite sex

Positive Action

Positive discrimination and positive action are often confused. Positive discrimination to favour one sex is illegal. The limited exceptions that allow discrimination in training, or encouragement to apply for work in which members of one sex are under-represented are usually referred to as 'positive action'.

Further information on the Sex Discrimination Act is available from the Equal Opportunities Commission or the Equality Commission for Northern Ireland (contact details can be found in the Appendix).

It is also useful for employers to know about the Equal Pay Act 1970 and Equal Pay (Amendment) Act 1983, or the Equal Pay Act (Northern Ireland) 1970 (amended 1984). This gives an individual a right to the same contractual pay and benefits as a person of the opposite sex in the same employment where s/he is doing like work, or work rated as equivalent under an analytical job evaluation study, or work that is proved to be of equal value. Victimisation because someone has tried to exercise their rights under the Equal Pay Act is prohibited. Further information is available from the Equal Opportunities Commission or the Equality Commission for Northern Ireland (contact details can be found in the Appendix).

Race Relations Act 1976 and Race Relations (Amendment) Act 2000

This legislation applies to all men, women and children in England, Wales and Scotland. Northern Ireland has its own equivalent legislation – Race Relations (Northern Ireland) Order 1997 and Fair Employment and Treatment (Northern Ireland) Order 1998. It prohibits direct and indirect discrimination and segregation on racial grounds in areas of employment, education, housing, and the provision of goods, facilities, and services. Victimisation because someone has tried to exercise their rights under the Act, or supported someone who has, is prohibited. Discriminatory advertisements are unlawful, as is instructing or pressurising others to discriminate on racial grounds, along with inciting people to racial hatred.

Changes were made to the Race Relations Act 1976 to strengthen it and extend its scope, not to replace it. The amended Act covers all employers, no matter how small; all schools (maintained and independent), colleges and universities; anyone providing goods, facilities and services to the public including selling, letting or managing property. As well as making it unlawful to discriminate on the grounds of race, colour, nationality, or ethnic or national origin, the Race Relations (Amendment) Act 2000 gives public authorities a statutory duty to tackle the elimination of racial discrimination, and promote equality of opportunity and good race relations.

The law protects against racial discrimination, abuse, harassment or violence because it is concerned with people's actions and the effects of these actions. It does not protect against racial prejudice or racism, which are the result of opinions or beliefs. It is not necessary to show that someone intended to discriminate against you, just that the effect of their actions was that you were treated less well.

The main exceptions to the legislation are:

- anything done under statutory authority to comply with an Act of Parliament (no matter when it was passed), or rules/regulations made by government ministers under any law. For example, offering a place at a school preferred by parents is lawful, even if it is racially discriminatory, as it is required under education laws

- discrimination on religious grounds; but there may be protection under the Race Relations Act if discrimination is also on the grounds of nationality or ethnic origin

Direct discrimination

This occurs when someone is treated less favourably than another person in comparable circumstances on racial grounds. Racial grounds are defined as those of race, colour, nationality (including citizenship) or ethnic or national origins. An example of direct racial discrimination is refusing to employ someone because s/he is black.

Indirect discrimination

This occurs when a condition or practice is applied to everyone, but a considerably smaller proportion of people from one racial group are able to comply with it and it cannot be justified (regardless of race) to apply that condition/practice, so a person is disadvantaged as a result. Examples of indirect racial discrimination include informal, 'word of mouth' recruitment, as it is more likely to exclude a particular racial group; or the requirement to wear a cap as part of a school uniform, as this would exclude Sikh males who are required to wear a turban for religious reasons. Indirect discrimination does not have to be deliberate or conscious; unintentional actions can still be unlawful.

Segregation

If segregation from others occurs on racial grounds, this is considered to be less favourable treatment, as defined by direct discrimination. An example would be grouping children according to their racial origins and for no other reason.

Discrimination in employment

In general it is unlawful to discriminate on racial grounds in recruitment and selection, treatment at work (including pay and benefits) or dismissal. The law applies to employment agencies as well as employers regardless of size and covers vocational trainees as well as employees. Trade unions and bodies responsible for conferring qualifications are also covered by the legislation.

Employees and potential employees have rights under the Race Relations Act whatever their length of employment and whatever hours are worked. Exceptions include:

- when encouraging job/training applications from people of a particular racial group, where it can be shown that such people are underrepresented in that specific work

- in the selection or treatment of employees where being from a specific racial group is a 'genuine occupational qualification'; for example, where the assistance of a member of that group who understands its language, customs, culture, religious practices etc., would enable the most effective provision for children of that racial group

- when employing someone to work in a private household for example, a nanny or au pair

Discrimination in education

Schools (whether state or independent), colleges and universities, early years provision and local education authorities must not discriminate on racial grounds in the ways they admit or treat pupils or students. Treatment includes exclusion.

Discrimination in housing

In general it is unlawful for anyone selling, letting or managing property (including business premises) to discriminate on racial grounds in the terms on which the premises are offered, by refusing purchase or different treatment from others who wish to buy/rent and by eviction. Exceptions include:

- owner-occupiers selling or letting property if they do not advertise or use an estate agent

- rental accommodation in 'small premises' where the owner also lives and would have to share facilities with people who are not members of the household

Discrimination in the provision of goods, facilities, and services

Generally, it is unlawful to discriminate on racial grounds in the provision of goods, facilities, and services by refusing services or providing them on less favourable terms. Exceptions include:

- clubs, associations and charities set up for people of a particular ethnic/national group (NB discrimination based on colour remains prohibited)

- taking in and caring for foster children or elderly people

- when taking action to meet the special needs of a particular racial group, for example, provision of bilingual practitioners, or halal catering

Under the Race Relations (Amendment) Act 2000, employment related complaints need to be filed at an employment tribunal within three months and other racial discrimination complaints need to be filed at a county or sheriff court within six months.

Positive Action

Positive discrimination or affirmative action is not allowed under race relations legislation. Thus, employers cannot try to change the balance of their workforce by selecting someone mainly because s/he is from a particular racial group. However, it is legal to take positive action to prevent discrimination or overcome past discrimination in employment, training and education and to meet specific welfare needs of members of a particular racial group. The aim of positive action is to ensure that people from previously excluded ethnic minority groups can compete on equal terms with others. The idea behind it is to make up for the accumulated effects of past discrimination.

The Commission for Racial Equality has a Code of Practice in Employment and an Education Code of Practice for England and Wales which provides guidance on the elimination of racial discrimination in education; both of which may prove useful to employers.

The Race Relations (Amendment) Act 2000 requires public authorities to provide fair and accessible services and to improve equal opportunities in employment. Under the legislation there is a general duty and specific duties on all major public bodies. The general duty is to make the promotion of racial equality central to their work and take account of racial equality in the day-to-day work of policymaking, service delivery, employment practice and other functions. The specific duties are to help them meet the general duty of the Act.

Under the Race Relations (Amendment) Act 2000, the Commission for Racial Equality has the power to conduct both named person and general investigations. While the Act gives the Commission for Racial Equality specific powers to conduct formal investigations, it also imposes obligations to safeguard respondents' interests, including publishing terms of reference.

Further information on the Race Relations Act 1976 and Race Relations (Amendment) Act 2000 is available from the Commission for Racial Equality (contact details can be found in the Appendix). Further information on the Race Relations (Northern Ireland) Order 1997, and Fair Employment and Treatment (Northern Ireland) Order 1998 is available from the Equality Commission for Northern Ireland (contact details can be found in the Appendix).

Disability Discrimination Act 1995

This law applies to all men, women and children in England, Wales and Scotland. Northern Ireland has its own equivalent legislation – Disability Discrimination Act 1995 and Equality (Disability etc.) (Northern Ireland) Order 2000. It deals with discrimination against people with disabilities in the areas of employment; provision of goods, facilities, services; and management, buying or renting of land or property. Victimisation is also prohibited. The Act covers any disability if it will last for at least 12 months (or has done so in the past) and, regardless of the ways the person has previously coped, it has a substantial effect on her/his ability to carry out normal day-to-day activities. Additionally, the Act requires education establishments to provide information for people with disabilities and allows the Government to set minimum standards to help people with disabilities use public transport easily.

The Disability Discrimination Act 1995 defines disability as a physical or mental impairment which has a substantial and long term adverse effect upon a person's ability to carry out normal day-to-day activities. It is useful to be clear about the scope of some of the words and terms used in this definition. The Act explains 'impairment', 'substantial', 'long-term' and 'day-to-day activities' as follows:

- impairment - this covers physical and mental impairments resulting from illness, accident or birth. Physical impairments affect the senses, for example, sight, hearing; mental impairments include learning disabilities and mental illness (if recognised by a respected body of medical opinion)

- substantial - for an effect to be substantial it does not have to be severe, but it must be more than minor or trivial, for example, inability to:
    turn taps or knobs
    remember and relay a simple message correctly
    see moving traffic clearly enough to cross a road safely

- long-term - this includes effects that have lasted, or are likely to last, at least 12 months or are likely to last for the rest of the life of the person affected. It also includes effects that are both likely to reoccur and likely to reoccur at least once after the 12 month period following first occurrence

- day-to-day activities - these are normal activities carried out by most people on a regular basis and must involve one of the following broad categories:

  mobility – moving from place to place
  manual dexterity, for example, use of the hands
  physical coordination
  continence
  ability to lift, carry or move ordinary objects
  speech, hearing or eyesight
  memory or ability to concentrate, learn or understand
  being able to recognise physical danger

The ability to work is not included as no particular form of work is 'normal' for most people. When considering the effects of a disability, focus on the condition and what it would be like without any medical treatment or equipment (for example, a hearing aid). The only exception is where poor eyesight is improved by wearing glasses/contact lenses; then the effects that count are those that remain even with the glasses/lenses.

The Act outlines specific information for the following cases or conditions:

- severe disfigurements
- impairments helped by treatment or artificial aids that is, artificial limbs, hearing aids
- progressive conditions, for example, cancer, HIV, multiple sclerosis, muscular dystrophy
- genetic dispositions
- past disabilities
- registered
- babies and children under the age of six

For the purposes of the Disability Discrimination Act the following conditions are not treated as impairments:

- addiction to, or dependency on, alcohol, nicotine or any other substance (unless the result of being medically prescribed)
- seasonal allergic rhinitis (for example, hayfever), except where it aggravates the effect of another condition
- tattoos and non-medical piercings
- a tendency to:

  set fires
  steal
  physical or sexual abuse of others

- exhibitionism
- voyeurism

Discrimination in employment

If an employer treats someone less favourably than others, or they refuse to make a reasonable adjustment, they are legally obliged to give a material and substantial reason. Exceptions include:

- an employer of less than 15 (full or part time) people

- some jobs, for example, prison officer, firefighter, members of the police force

The Act does not prevent employers from making arrangements that provide more favourable treatment to people with disabilities. In fact, some charities set up to help people with a particular disability and organisations offering supported employment may discriminate in favour of certain disabled applicants and employees.

Employers should make adjustments to employment arrangements, for example, flexible working hours, or physical workplace features, so as not to put a disabled person at a substantial disadvantage. Adjustments should be made when the employer becomes aware of the disability.

Discrimination in the provision of goods, facilities, and services

Generally, it is unlawful to discriminate on the grounds of disability in the provision of goods, facilities and services to the public by treating some less favourably because of their disability, or not making reasonable adjustments to the way the service is delivered to enable use. This applies to the private, public and voluntary sectors and there are no size exemptions. Exceptions include:

- education
- transport
- services not available to the public, for example, those provided by private clubs for their members

Under the Act providers of services must 'take reasonable steps' to:

- change policies, practices or procedures that make it impossible or reasonably difficult for people with disabilities to use a service

- provide an auxiliary aid or service which would enable people with disabilities to use a service

- overcome physical barriers which make it impossible or unreasonably difficult for people with disabilities to use a service by providing it by a reasonably alternative method

From 2004, service providers have to take reasonable steps to remove, alter or provide reasonable means of avoiding physical features which make it unreasonably difficult for people with disabilities to use a service.

The Disability Rights Commission produces Assessment Guides to help people decide if they have been discriminated against as, unfortunately there is much practice which, while not good nor desirable, is not illegal. It may be if the treatment experienced is not illegal, the person may wish to make a complaint under your organisation's complaints procedure. However, there are time limits for claims made under the Act: three months for employment related complaints and six months for other claims.

To help implement the Disability Discrimination Act three Codes of Practice were drawn up for use by courts and employment tribunals in legal proceedings under the Act. These are, Code of Practice for:

- Elimination of Discrimination in the Field of Employment Against Disabled Persons or Persons who have had a Disability

- Rights of Access to Goods, Facilities, Services and Premises

- Duties of Trade Organisations to their Disabled Members and Applicants

Under the Disability Discrimination Act 1995, the Disability Rights Commission has a number of statutory duties to:

- work to eliminate discrimination against people with disabilities
- promote equal opportunities for people with disabilities
- encourage good practice in the treatment of people with disabilities
- advise Government on the working of disability legislation

Although the Disability Rights Commission seeks to educate the public and work in partnership with employers and service providers, it does have statutory enforcement powers, including the power to:

- conduct formal investigations
- serve non-discrimination notices
- enter into an agreement with a person who undertakes not to commit any further unlawful acts
- act over persistent discrimination
- provide assistance to an individual bringing proceedings over unlawful discrimination
- issue codes of practice
- arrange for conciliation of disputes

Further information on the Disability Discrimination Act 1995 is available from the Disability Rights Commission (contact details can be found in the Appendix). Further information on the Disability Discrimination Act 1995 and Equality (Disability etc.) (Northern Ireland) Order 2000 is available from the Equality Commission for Northern Ireland (contact details can be found in the Appendix).

It is also necessary for early years education providers to know about the Code of Practice on the Identification and Assessment of Children with Special Educational Needs (SEN) or Manual of Good Practice in Special Educational Needs in Scotland. With the exception of Scotland, this is commonly known as the Code of Practice and was last revised in 2001. It sets out guidelines for every local education authority and school to follow. If parents feel they have grounds for concern they can take a complaint to a court or tribunal which will investigate, but its decisions are not legally binding. The Secretary of State for Education can only recommend the action to be taken by a local authority.

The Code of Practice requires early years education providers to identify a member of staff to undertake the role of Special Educational Needs Coordinator (SENCO). The SENCO is responsible for:

- the day-to-day operation of the provider's SEN policy
- coordinating provision for children with SEN within their provision
- maintaining the SEN register and overseeing relevant records on all children with SEN
- liaising with parents of children with SEN
- contributing to in-service training of staff
- liaising with external agencies, for example, Educational Psychology service, medical and social services, support agencies

Further information on the Code of Practice or Manual of Good Practice is available from the Department for Education and Skills (DfES), the Scottish Executive, Welsh Assembly, or Northern Ireland Executive (contact details can be found in the Appendix) or your local education authority.

It is also useful for early years education providers to know about the Special Educational Needs and Disability Rights in Education Act 2001. This changes existing legislation in the Education Act 1996 and strengthens the right of children with SEN to be educated in mainstream schools. There is also a duty on local education authorities and schools to not treat disabled pupils less favourably, without justification, for a reason which relates to their disability and to make reasonable adjustments so disabled pupils are not put at a substantial disadvantage compared to pupils who are not disabled. Further information is available from the Department for Education and Skills (DfES) (contact details can be found in the Appendix).

Reflection

Do I need to make any changes to my practice?

-
-
-

What help and support do I need to change my practice?

-
-
-

What further information do I need and where can I get this?

-
-
-

How do I actively include people who experience prejudice, discrimination, harassment and/or stereotyping?

-
-
-

Summary

Much equal opportunities work is about examining and changing personal attitudes and, often, challenging other people's attitudes. Many workers look for specific ideas which they can use in their practice. While specific solutions may be quick and easy, and make practitioners feel safe that they are doing things correctly, it is possible that they may lead to tokenism. This can be dangerous as it does not treat people as individuals and, as ideas change, leaves practitioners feeling confused, under-confident, open to accusations of prejudice and discriminatory practice and potentially disillusioned. However, if the principles of equal opportunities are understood, it is possible to find appropriate solutions specific to the individual (child or adult) with whom you are dealing. It also means that ideas and resources to promote equal opportunities can be used in context with the current experiences and opportunities being encountered by children and adults.

Working towards equal opportunities is a requirement of all early years practitioners. This can raise different and, sometimes, difficult issues for many practitioners and the people with whom they work. Some may feel:

- uncomfortable because it raises issues with which they would rather not deal – they feel very threatened about examining their own attitudes

- it is an issue they know they should address but do not know where to start or, more often, are afraid of getting it wrong

- it is an issue that does not affect young children

- they are already working within an appropriate equal opportunities framework

Everyone has some sort of thoughts about the many different groups represented in society. It is a natural part of life to hold opinions and have attitudes, and they are developed from a variety of sources including parents, the media (newspapers, radio, and television) and friends. Attitudes and opinions can be expressed in actions, language or behaviour. Some attitudes and opinions are regarded as positive and healthy, others as negative and unhealthy; some may be based on a stereotype or prejudice.

Children develop their attitudes from the environment around them; the toys they play with, the television programmes and videos they watch, advertising, the books they read (or are read to them) and the attitudes of the adults with whom they have contact. Television can have a profound effect on children and research has found by the time children are 12 they have spent more time watching television than they have spent at school. Background knowledge about child development may help you further understand how children develop their own attitudes and opinions.

As mentioned in Section 2, 'What about me?', young children do develop attitudes towards both colour and gender in particular, and these may be discriminatory attitudes. As the environment can give children discriminatory messages about groups and individuals in society, it is important to address equal opportunities in all areas of practice. Contact with people, for example, those of a different sex, race or ability, does not on its own reduce misconceptions or fear. There is still a need for active learning about different people among adults and children, in an environment that promotes equal opportunities.

Where and whenever you work with children, it is important that all equal opportunities issues are addressed and you work towards challenging and eliminating prejudice and discrimination. As a role model you influence how children develop their own attitudes and opinions. Equal opportunities should be addressed in all areas of your practice with children, parents and colleagues. This is sometimes known as working within an 'anti-discriminatory framework'. It is necessary for all early years practitioners to address these issues and ensure it is not left to one or two people.

There are three strands to equal opportunities practice - equality of opportunity, anti-discrimination work, and celebrating diversity:

Equality of opportunity – having equal access to opportunities to learn and develop and so an individual can work towards realising her/his potential. The individuality of a person should be respected and therefore people should not be treated all the same; to meet individual needs, it is necessary to treat people with 'equal concern', giving the appropriate support (whether this be 'more' or 'different' support) to ensure equality of opportunity. Avoid stereotyping people on any basis, as stereotypes act as barriers to equality of access to opportunity. By actively demonstrating you value individuals' personal characteristics you help her/him develop and maintain self-esteem.

Anti-discrimination work – all people should acknowledge and address any personal beliefs or opinions which prevent them from respecting others. Plus, they need to comply with legislation and their workplace policies relating to discrimination. In addition, early years practitioners need to be mindful of the fact that children learn prejudice at a very early age, so must provide them with accurate information to help them avoid prejudice, as well as challenging all expressions of prejudice, whether from children or adults, along with offering support to those who are objects of prejudice and discrimination.

Celebrating diversity – this is one of the most common ways of demonstrating compliance with equal opportunities ideas. Many early years settings find that providing information about a variety of traditions, customs and festivals is relatively easy, particularly if they operate in an ethnically diverse area. It can be argued this is even more important in areas where there are few members of minority ethnic groups and also that the term should not be confined to racial diversity. In addition, early years practitioners need to be mindful of helping children to develop a sense of identity within their racial, cultural and social groups as well as providing opportunities to learn about other cultures. It is worth remembering pride in one's own cultural and social background does not require condemnation of that of others.

In short, good practice in equal opportunities includes:

- making all people feel valued and good about themselves

- treating people with individual and equal concern

- ensuring everyone is included

- enabling people to share their experiences with each other

- actively promoting non-stereotypical behaviour

- actively promoting racial, cultural and religious diversity

- appreciating and valuing people's differences and similarities

Even where good equal opportunities practice is promoted and followed there can still be incidents of discriminatory behaviour. A written policy will create a framework within which practitioners can work, but this is not enough. It is necessary to have procedures as to how the policy is going to be put into practice. Both policy and procedures should be valued and owned by all involved in their development and execution. When developing procedures, it is necessary to appreciate there is no single best way to do anything, a range of practices can be promoted. It would be beneficial to consider, your assumptions, behaviour, the language you use and be clear as to why some statements and ways of behaviour are unacceptable.

Additionally, it would be helpful to think about how you are going to challenge stereotyping and prejudice, tackle discrimination, respond to insulting behaviour and harassment, and promote tolerance. Plus, how you will encourage participation yet still respect individual/parental requests, for example, a Jehovah's Witness who does not wish to celebrate religious festivals. Also, consider the experiences and opportunities that can be developed and used to help children and adults learn it is unacceptable to make fun of any aspect of an individual's identity; and how to support all people to stand up for themselves.

It is helpful to have a strategy for dealing with discriminatory behaviour and/or disparaging remarks. In all such cases, every individual has a responsibility to act, otherwise s/he is adding to the offence and any hurt experienced. Most strategies involve responding by:

- actively listening to all sides of the story

- supporting the victim in the presence of the perpetrator

- informing the perpetrator, in the presence of the victim and others where possible, why her/his behaviour is unacceptable

- making it clear to all, especially the victim, that the action or behaviour is not excused, but taken very seriously and there is an expectation it will not happen again

- taking both immediate, and long term action

All people who breaks any rules you have regarding equal opportunities should have it made clear to them such behaviour is unacceptable. Remember, a perpetrator may need support too. So do not blame the perpetrator personally, challenge the issue not the person, support with explanations and thus s/he is more likely to change her/his ideas and behaviour.

It is important to remember one person cannot know everything. Parents and colleagues are a good resource and may be able to help with activities or provide information. There are also groups and government departments that provide advice, including Codes of Practice for employers (see Appendix). Some groups also provide training on equal opportunities issues, or can advise were this can be accessed. Ongoing training can help practitioners reflect on their values, attitudes and practices, and may provide an opportunity to learn how to challenge or handle different situations.

It is also important to appreciate sometimes mistakes will be made and not everything that is tried will work well the first time. This should not stop you from trying to work within an equal opportunities framework, but it is important that, when mistakes are made, you learn from them and do not just give up. For example, in good equal opportunities practice it is wise not to make assumptions of any kind; many bad experiences result from misunderstanding, or lack of understanding, on the part of any of the people involved in the experience. So, it is far better to clarify your concern by asking in a sensitive manner; this can take practice and therefore, time. It is also useful to develop both the ability to actively listen (compared to just hearing) and negotiate strategies. Again, this will take time, but keep trying, it will become easier to work within an equal opportunities framework, and your practice will be much improved.

Remember, for some people their sense of identity is strongly tied to their ethnic, racial, or cultural background, and/or nationality. Others may derive a stronger sense of identity from their sex/gender, or their degree of able-bodiedness. For most people their sense of identity is created from a mixture of all of these, but the dominant aspects vary from person to person. A person's sense of self is reinforced by others around her/him acknowledging her/his existence and lifestyle, actively listening to her/him and hearing what s/he has to say. Working towards equal opportunities will help children, families and colleagues to both value and respect all the groups in our diverse society and view people as individuals.

Finally, it is probably worth remembering that in dealing with any difference:

**The first thing you have to do is forget the difference;
the second is, you must never forget the difference.**

Reflection

How do I currently promote equal opportunities?

-
-
-

How do I feel I could further improve my personal practice?

-
-
-

What help and support may I need to change my personal practice?

-
-
-

What further training do I feel I need and where might I access this?

-
-
-

Appendix

This section outlines some of the key organisations and government departments that may be able to provide information, help and support in your equal opportunities work. It is not a comprehensive list of all relevant organisations and departments.

Contact details

Age Positive Team
Department for Work and Pensions
Room W8d
Moorfoot
Sheffield S1 4PQ
www.agepositive.gov.uk

Carers National Association
20-25 Glasshouse Yard
London
EC1A 4JT

The Princess Royal Trust for Carers
142 Minories
London
EC3N 1LB
www.carers.org

The Princess Royal Trust for Carers
215 West Campbell Street
Glasgow
G2 4TT
www.carers.org

Commission for Racial Equality
St Dunstans House
201-211 Borough High Street
London
SE1 1GZ
www.cre.gov.uk

Commission for Racial Equality (Scotland)
The Tun
12 Jackson's Entry
off Holyrood Road
Edinburgh
EH8 8PJ

Commission for Racial Equality (Wales)
3rd Floor
Capital Tower
Greyfrairs Road
Cardiff
CF10 3AG

Equality Commission for Northern Ireland
Equality House
7-9 Shaftesbury Square
Belfast
BT2 7DP
www.equalityni.org

Department for Education and Skills (DfES)
Great Smith Street
London
SW1P 3BT
www.dfes.gov.uk

Scotland Executive Education Department
Victoria Quay
Edinburgh
EH6 6QQ
www.scotland.gov.uk

National Assembly for Wales
Cathays Park
Cardiff
CF10 3NQ
www.wales .gov.uk

Department for Education Northern Ireland
Northern Ireland Executive
Rathgael House
43 Balloo Road
Bangor
County Down
BT19 7PR
www.deni.gov.uk

Office for Standards in Education (Ofsted)
Early Years Directorate
Alexandra House
33 Kingsway
London
WC2B 6SE
www.ofsted.gov.uk

Sure Start Unit
Caxton House
6-12 Tothill Street
London
SW1H 9NA
www.surestart.gov.uk

Disability Rights Commission
www.drc-gb.org

Equality Commission for Northern Ireland
Equality House
7-9 Shaftesbury Square
Belfast
BT2 7DP
www.equalityni.org

Equal Opportunities Commission
Arndale House
Arndale Centre
Manchester
M4 3EQ
www.eoc.org.uk

Equal Opportunities Commission Regional
Office
St Stephens House
279 Bath Street
Glasgow
G2 4JL

Equal Opportunities Commission Regional
Office
Windsor House
Windsor Lane
Cardiff
CF10 3GE

Equality Commission for Northern Ireland
Equality House
7-9 Shaftesbury Square
Belfast
BT2 7DP
www.equalityni.org

Human Rights Unit
Home Office
50 Queens Anne's Gate
London
SW1H 9AT
www.homeoffice.gov.uk/hract

The Human Rights Directorate
Office of the First Minister and Deputy
First Minister
Castle Buildings
Stormont
Belfast
BT4 3SG

Scottish Justice Department
Saughton House
Broomhouse Drive
Edinburgh
EH11 3XD

'Human Rights'
PEP Division
National Assembly for Wales
Crown Buildings
Cathays Park
Cardiff
CF10 3NQ
www.wales.gov.uk

National Association for the Care and Resettlement of Offenders
169 Clapham Road
London
SW9 0PU
www.nacro.org.uk

One Parent Families
255 Kentish Town Road
London NW5 2LX
www.opfs.org.uk

One Parent Families Scotland
13 Gayfield Square
Edinburgh
EH1 3NX
www.opfs.org.uk

Gingerbread
7 Sovereign Close
Sovereign Court
London
E1W 3HW
www.gingerbread.org.uk

Gingerbread Northern Ireland
169 University Street
Belfast
BT7 1HR
www.gingerbreadni.org

Gingerbread Scotland
1041 Argyle Street
Glasgow
G3 8LX
www.gingerbread.org.uk